LINUX

Everything you need to get started with Ubuntu Linux

LINUX

Everything you need to get started with Ubuntu Linux

Mike Saunders

Mike Saunders is a full-time Linux journalist, with over a decade of daily experience in using, administering and documenting the operating system. He has also written his own operating system (http://mikeos.berlios.de). He lives in Bath, England.

Photo by Lucia Paulikova

First published in December 2010

A catalogue record for this book is available from the British Library

ISBN 978 1 84425 970 0

Published by Haynes Publishing,
Sparkford, Yeovil, Somerset BA22 7JJ, UK

Tel: 01963 442030 Fax: 01963 440001
Int. tel: +44 1963 442030 Int. fax: +44 1963 440001
E-mail: sales@haynes.co.uk
Website: www.haynes.co.uk

Haynes North America, Inc.,
861 Lawrence Drive, Newbury Park,
California 91320, USA

Design and layout: Richard Parsons

Printed and bound in the USA

Contents

LINUX MANUAL
Introduction

Tux is the cheerful Linux mascot, dreamt up by Larry Ewing.

Stability. Security. Speed. The big three Ss in computing appear to have been long forgotten, replaced by the apathetic acceptance that PCs break down and have problems because, well, that's just the way things are. How many times have you heard conversations like this?

– 'Hey, the PC has crashed again!'
– 'Never mind, just reboot it.'

Or even worse, this?

– 'For some reason everything is slowing to a crawl.'
– 'Have you bought the latest virus checker updates?'

PCs crash and need virus checkers, right? Let's just accept that and spend the requisite hours every week cleaning up problems, buying new temporary fixes and hoping that the next wave of updates will magically solve everything.

Actually, let's not. It turns out that there is a solution, and it doesn't involve spending a stack of money on a Mac (and then dealing with its own range of issues). There's a solution born out of the Internet, put together by full-time programmers, part-type hobby coders and everyday users. A totally free solution created for the love of good, reliable computing. A solution for everyone who wants a fresh start with computers.

Welcome to Linux.

Welcome to an operating system that's completely free of charge, and free to share with your friends, colleagues and anyone else. If they like it, just give them a copy. This isn't shareware, or trialware, or adware or anything like that – it's completely open and explicitly created so that everyone can share it and improve it.

Linux is reliable. In fact, extremely reliable. In November 2009, every single one of the top ten fastest supercomputers in the world was running Linux. Google's massive infrastructure is built on tens of thousands of servers running Linux. It's huge in the web server market, huge in academia, and huge wherever stability is a key issue.

Linux is also secure. You don't need a virus checker, or malware detector, or spyware killer, or anything like that. Linux was designed from the ground up for the Internet, so right from the start it had precautions in place to stop random programs overwriting system files. It includes powerful security mechanisms to keep your data safe, and because it's completely open and free, nobody can sneak in malicious code without the rest of the world knowing.

But above all, as you'll see as we install and explore it, Linux is fun. It's different, impressively designed, stimulating and rich with great technology and features. It has both serious high-end software and lunchtime-distraction games. It's a whole world of safe, fast and rock-solid computing, and reaching more and more users every day.

Welcome to the future.

From bedroom hackers...

The first question everyone asks when they hear about Linux is: 'Why is this free?' And given the vast amount of money made in the software industry, it's a very valid question. But to answer it properly, we need to step back a while to 1983.

Richard Matthew Stallman was a programmer in the MIT Computer Science and Artificial Intelligence Laboratory in Cambridge, Massachusetts, USA. A prolific software engineer, Stallman observed a decline in software freedom that was taking place in the late 1970s and early 1980s. Previously, sharing the source code of a program – that is, the original, human-readable recipe for a program – was simply the done thing. Programmers loved to exchange information and ideas without financial restrictions.

Richard Stallman, tireless campaigner for software freedom and original developer of GNU. (Photo: CC-SA, NicoBZH on Flickr)

As the computer software market emerged, however, many developers stopped supplying source code with their programs. As a customer, you only received the closed, locked-down binary version of the software – much like buying a car with the bonnet welded shut. This is the situation with Windows and many other programs today. For many users this lack of access to the internals wasn't an issue, but for those programmers who had grown up with the spirit of sharing ideas and code, these were bad times.

Stallman couldn't stand by and watch these freedoms be eroded. While he wasn't against the idea of people getting rich, he resented the fact that companies were charging money for access to source code; in other words, that the spirit of community, the free exchange of ideas and sharing help with your friends and colleagues, was being increasingly dictated (and limited) by the men with the money.

So, Stallman had a plan. For years he had been using Unix, a powerful operating system that was generally confined to mainframes, minicomputers and other high-end systems (as opposed to the extremely simple DOS that people were using on home PCs). He decided to create his own version of Unix, called GNU (standing for GNU's Not Unix – a recursive acronym). GNU would be completely free, with the source code available for anyone to share, change and improve without money being an issue.

He created a licence that guaranteed these freedoms: the GNU General Public Licence (aka GPL). A program using this licence is 'Free Software' (the capital F highlighting that it's free as in freedom, and not just price), and will always be Free. No company can take the source code, change it and distribute their own binary-only version – they must also give away their source code changes.

...to ten thousand google servers

By 1991, GNU was doing fairly well, with lots of developers around the Internet involved and many components of the operating system complete. However, GNU was still lacking a kernel – the core component of an operating system, which talks to hardware, makes sure each program has enough memory and so forth. Meanwhile, a Finnish computing student called Linus Torvalds was working on his own kernel purely as a personal research project. He had been using some GNU tools but never intended his work to be 'big and professional like GNU'.

The Internet decided otherwise, however. When Torvalds released his Linux kernel, various groups mixed it together with more GNU tools and programs from other projects, and a surprisingly powerful operating system emerged. (Many call it GNU/Linux for this reason.) At first, bedroom-dwelling programmers and students used Linux to understand how operating systems worked.

As years went by, companies saw it as a free alternative to the expensive, closed versions of Unix still in use, and

Linus Torvalds, Finnish superprogrammer and creator of the Linux kernel. (Photo: GFDL, Martin Streicher)

added their own features and updates (sending their work to Torvalds for inclusion). Some developers thought that the term 'Free Software' could dissuade commercial entities from getting involved, so they promoted an alternative, 'Open Source', which focused on the practical benefits of fully available source code.

Indeed, there were many benefits. Because the complete source code was available, bugs and security problems were spotted and fixed extremely quickly. Any Linux user in the world could look through the code and find potential problems – in stark contrast to Windows, for which most users only have the binary, black magic machine code. Businesses saw huge advantages in adopting an OS they could fully customise, rather than having to awkwardly bolt on components to someone else's (closed) system.

Many Linux-based companies sprang up throughout the 1990s and the OS grew from a bunch of part-time coders having fun to a broad, serious, industrial-strength operating system. Linux magazines started to appear. PC users were talking about it. Google was building an entire business on it. Huge companies such as IBM contribute manpower to Linux, writing code, adding features and writing documentation.

'Open Source' was created as an alternative term for 'Free Software', to appeal more to businesses.

Yet brilliantly, the initial spirit still prevails today: anyone can get the source code from the Internet, start exploring and make changes. Many of the updates and new features in Linux come from people casually tinkering with it on their home PCs. Meanwhile, Richard Stallman continues to press home the importance of freedom and sharing, and Linus Torvalds has the final say in the kernel, still loving programming and doing what he does 'just for fun'.

The many sources of Linux

It's important to note that Linux, as a whole operating system, is developed by many different groups. Some work on the kernel, some on the graphical interface, and some on the development tools. There are scattered communities around the Internet: for instance, www.kernel.org is the home of kernel development, with links to source code, mailing lists and documentation. Over at www.gnome.org programmers are working on the graphical side of the OS. There are hundreds of other communities working on their own projects.

Technically, it is possible to grab each of these components individually and assemble them together into a full Linux operating system – indeed, a project called Linux From Scratch explains how to do just that. However, it's extremely time-consuming, highly technical and many

www.gnome.org is the home of Gnome development, one of the user interfaces used by Linux.

things can go wrong along the way. Consequently, we have 'distributions' of Linux: pre-compiled, ready-to-go versions of the operating system with all the hard work already done.

Who can make a distribution (or 'distro')? Anyone with the required knowledge is free to make their own OS – Bob's Linux, Super Turbo Mega Linux, or anything else. There are hundreds of Linux distributions in existence, ranging from one-man hobby projects to major, commercially backed

If you have an old PC sitting around doing nothing, breathe new life into it with a lightweight distro.

Linux Manual

systems for enterprise use, and many in between. This flexibility is another major plus point for Linux – if you want a version of Linux tailored for children, it exists. If you want a lightweight distro for that old Pentium I box in the attic, it exists. If you're not interested in a graphical interface and just want to serve web pages... yes, it exists. Many distros begin life as 'forks' or spin-offs of other distros.

In the Appendix you'll find a list of the 30 most important Linux distributions, what they do and where you can find them. However, one particular distribution has risen rapidly to the top in the last five years: Ubuntu Linux. Named after a southern African philosophy espousing humanity towards others, and launched by one-time astronaut Mark Shuttleworth, Ubuntu has been enormously successful, bringing millions of new users to Linux. Whereas some Linux distributions focus on particular niches, Ubuntu aims for the general home and office desktop, taking the fight directly to Windows and Mac OS X.

Android is Google's rapidly growing operating system for smartphones, based on Linux.

Getting ready

So, we know what Linux is, where it has come from and why it's growing so rapidly. The next step is to install it. Ubuntu Linux is included on the CD provided with this book, and gives you a complete Linux installation with office tools, Internet software, games and much more. Best of all, you don't have to remove Windows to install it: Ubuntu lets you set up a dual-boot system so that you can have both Windows and Linux on the same hard drive. You simply choose the OS you want to run when your PC starts. (Of course, if you want to move away from Windows completely, you can tell the Linux installer that you want it to be the only operating system on your hard drive.)

Through the course of this book we'll show you how to install Linux, explore the desktop, and master the included Internet, office and multimedia software. You'll learn how to get on the Internet, customise the web browser, create documents and share files with Microsoft Office users. Then we'll look at system administration topics –

adding new users, configuring hardware and getting software updates – before explaining how to run your own web server and start programming on Linux. At the end you'll find a handy glossary of terms used in the Linux world, along with a reference guide for essential commands.

You'll progress from the level of Linux novice to a very confident user with the knowledge to use and adapt Linux in every situation. You'll feel at home with the operating system and have the skills to explore new distributions and fix problems if you encounter them. And best of all, you'll be fully empowered to spread the word of Linux and Free Software, giving your friends, family and colleagues stress-free computing (and saving them lots of money at the same time).

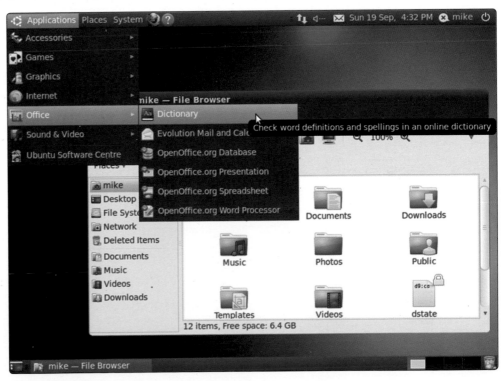

A screen shot showing the desktop from Ubuntu Linux in all its glory.

01. Installation

In this section

INSTALLATION
Getting prepared

Installing a new operating system may initially appear to be a major task – a brain transplant for your computer, in a way. Many computer users have never installed an operating system before, always using whatever was pre-installed with the machine they bought (usually Windows). If you've been using computers for a while, chances are you've gone through the tiresome Windows installation process a few times, and you're not particularly looking forward to this initial phase of your Linux experience.

Well, worry not. Linux is much, much easier to install than Windows for three reasons:

1 It doesn't require serial numbers or validation keys or Windows Activation Genuine Advantage Pro or anything like that.
2 It includes a huge number of hardware drivers – you almost certainly won't have to hunt down driver packs.
3 It doesn't think it should be the only operating system on your hard drive, and therefore peacefully coexists with other OSs.

Ubuntu Linux is supplied on a single CD-ROM.

The first thing to do is check your PC against Ubuntu's minimum hardware requirements:

■ **Memory:** 256MB RAM. Note that this needs to be dedicated, free RAM. If your graphics card uses shared memory, for instance, it will take away free RAM from this number and you'll end up with less. 256MB is the bare minimum, but we recommend 512MB for smooth running.

■ **Processor:** Intel or AMD-compatible x86 or x86-64 CPU, 800MHz. That's enough speed for basic office work and web browsing. For more demanding tasks such as high definition video, we recommend a minimum 2GHz CPU. The version of Ubuntu on the disc included with this book is 32-bit, but it will run happily on both 32-bit and 64-bit PCs.

Linux supports almost every video, sound and network card you can find, and is generally very good at detecting printers and scanners too. USB and PS/2 keyboards and mice all work, along with USB game controllers, USB external hard drives (or flash drives) and many other peripherals.

In terms of hard drive space, Linux is a standalone operating system and not a normal program, so it needs dedicated space on your hard drive. The installer, which we'll come to in a moment, lets you create this space. We recommend allocating at least 10GB for Linux – the Ubuntu installation takes up less than 2.5GB, but you will want extra room for your personal files.

Now, how you go about allocating this space depends on what you want to do with your hard drive.

If you're happy to devote the entire drive to Linux, that's very easy: back up any important data and the installer will wipe your drive clean and use it in its entirety for Linux. If you're currently running Windows, however, and you want to keep Windows on the drive, you can set up a 'dual-boot' system. This shrinks the Windows part of the disk to make room for Linux, and installs a new boot loader so that when you turn on your PC you can choose whether to start Ubuntu Linux or Windows.

If you are going to use the dual-boot option, it is absolutely vital that you back up important data in Windows before starting the installation! It's extremely unlikely that anything will go wrong, but you will be changing the layout of your hard drive, so backing up data (and running any disk scanning and disk defragmenter tools if possible) before starting the installer is hugely important.

So, if you're ready to go, let's do this!

INSTALLATION
Performing the installation

1 Booting the CD

Inside this book you'll find a CD of Ubuntu Linux 10.04. This contains the full operating system, and needs to be loaded directly when your PC starts. Insert the CD into your drive and start (or restart if you're in Windows) your machine. Many modern PCs and laptops are configured to check for a CD or DVD when they start up, and begin loading the operating system on the optical media. If, after a few moments and some CD activity, you see the Ubuntu logo on the screen, congratulations – it worked.

If not, and your PC starts booting Windows instead, it means that your system isn't configured to boot from the CD/DVD drive. To fix this you will need to change the settings in your BIOS, which is the mini operating system and hardware-checking software built into your PC. Restart your machine and look at the very first messages that appear – you will see something like 'F12 Settings' or 'Press Esc for BIOS setup' or similar. Hit the appropriate key to open the BIOS settings. (If you can't see any information or you're not sure, look at your PC's manual.)

In the BIOS screen, search for the option to change the boot order of drives connected to your system. The method varies from BIOS to BIOS, but in most cases you'll find a 'Boot' category with a list of drives. The PC checks the first drive for an operating system, then the second, and so forth. You need to change it so that the CD/DVD drive is the first in the list (the keys to move items should be displayed at the bottom).

When you're done, exit the BIOS and the PC will restart, loading Ubuntu from the CD/DVD drive.

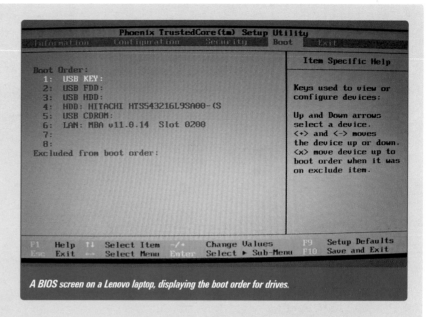

A BIOS screen on a Lenovo laptop, displaying the boot order for drives.

2 The installer appears

After a few moments, the first screen of the installer should appear. (If not, and you're sure that the machine is definitely booting from the CD, look at the end of this section for other boot options to try.) Ubuntu's installer is a straightforward step-by-step utility that asks you a few questions and automates the process as much as possible.

In this screen you can select your language. As you're reading this book then you'll almost certainly want English, but if you scroll down the list you can see how much work has been put in by the international Ubuntu community. So, select your language and click the Install Ubuntu 10.04 LTS button. (We'll cover the other button, Try Ubuntu, later.)

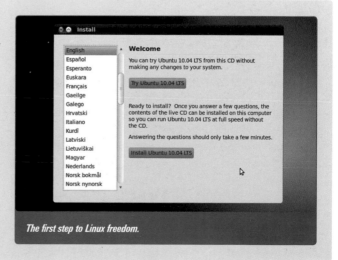

The first step to Linux freedom.

3 Choosing your location

In the next screen you'll see a map, prompting you to set your location:

Click on the map to choose the nearest location to where you are, or use the drop-down boxes beneath the map. This is an important step, as it determines localisation settings (eg whether to use pounds, dollars or Euros) in your new Linux system.

When you're done, click Forward.

Pinpoint your position on the planet.

4 Choose your keyboard layout

The installer will then ask you to set your keyboard layout:

The suggested option will be based on the location you chose in the previous step, but if you want to change it, click on the 'Choose your own' button and select it from the list.

Keyboard settings.

5 Partitioning your drive

Now we come to the biggest and most important step: allocating space for Linux on your hard drive.

The bar at the top of the screen shows the current layout of your hard drive. If it's a brand new drive with no operating system installed, this bar will be empty; if you have Windows installed and it's using up all of the space on the drive, it will be filled with blue as in this screenshot.

Beneath that you have three options. If you want to keep Windows and set up a dual-boot system as described earlier, in which you'll see a menu when your computer starts, choose the first option, 'Install them side by side'. Beneath the options is another bar with a slider in the middle. You can click and drag the slider to choose how much of your hard drive will be devoted to Windows, and how much to Ubuntu. We recommend giving at least 10GB to Linux – but the more space the better! Once you're happy with the amounts, click Forward and move on to Step 7.

If you want to format your hard drive and allocate all of its space to Linux, or if you have a second hard drive and want to install Linux on it, leaving the first drive intact, choose the second option, 'Erase and use the entire disk'.

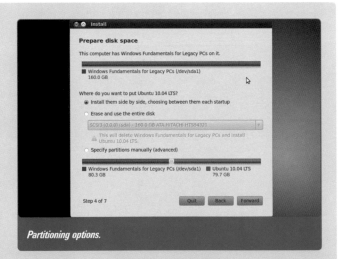

Partitioning options.

Select the drive that you want to install Ubuntu on, and click Forward. (One last reminder: this will wipe everything from the drive, so if you haven't backed up important data, reboot into Windows and save it now!) Then go on to Step 7.

There is one other option, 'Specify partitions manually', which you won't need to consider in your first install. For your future reference we'll cover it here in Step 6, but there's no need to read it now.

6 Manual partitioning
Here's what you'll see if you choose the advanced partitioning option:

The layout will vary depending on the structure of your drive, but the concepts will be the same. You have a list of partitions (areas) on your hard drive. Those marked with 'ntfs' as the type are for Windows. At a minimum, Linux needs a root partition to store its files, along with a swap partition for virtual memory.

You can click on an NTFS partition and the Change button to resize it, then click in the 'free space' option in the list and Add to create a new partition. For the root partition, which is somewhat like the C: drive in Windows, create a primary partition of minimum 10000MB with the Ext4 file system and '/' (forward slash) as the mount point. Then add another new partition in the free space of the size of your RAM (but no larger than 2GB), and choose 'swap area' as the type.

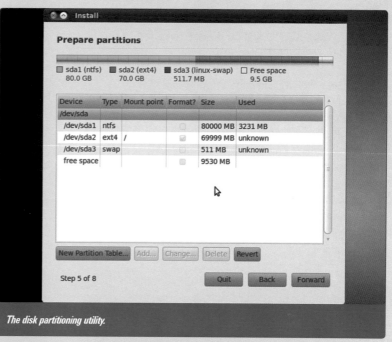

The disk partitioning utility.

Click Forward to save the changes to the disk and continue, or Revert to go back to the previous partitioning scheme.

7 Creating a user account
Next up is the user account step:

For the sake of security, everyone on a Linux machine has to be identifiable. You don't simply land in a magic administrator role like old Windows releases – you have to log in as a normal user, and that limits you to doing certain things for security reasons. For instance, as a normal user you can't delete system files or break the workings of the system; this helps to eliminate viruses, trojans and other security problems. Whenever you do perform a task that requires more rights (aka administrator privileges), such as installing software, you'll be asked for your password.

On this screen, enter your full name along with a short, single-word login name (aka username). Then enter a password and confirm that it's correct. Ubuntu will let you know whether your password is weak, fair or strong – if it's too weak, try adding extra numbers to the end. Note that passwords are case-sensitive, so if you ever have a problem logging in, make sure that the Caps Lock key isn't activated!

You can also provide a name for the computer to determine how it will be seen on the network, and also choose whether to log in automatically when Ubuntu boots or asks for your username and password at the login

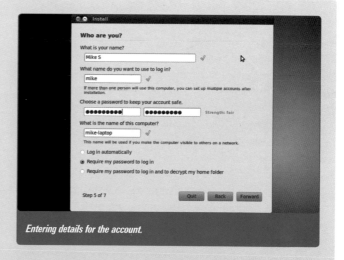

Entering details for the account.

screen. There's also an option to decrypt your home folder when you log in: if you activate this, your personal files will be encrypted and therefore if anyone manages to get hold of your hard drive, they won't be able to access your data without knowing your password. There is a small performance impact for enabling this, but it's a good idea if you're installing Linux on a business laptop that will be used in public places and has a chance of being stolen.

When you're done, click Forward.

8 Windows migration

This step will only appear if you're creating a dual-boot system with Windows:

Ubuntu's installer will scan the Windows partition on the hard drive and look for user accounts and files on it. Then it will ask you if you want to recreate these accounts in the new Linux installation. This is a quick way to get up-and-running with your existing data, without having to fiddle around in the file manager or copy it across via an external drive.

Choose the accounts, files and settings you want transfered by clicking in the boxes, and then click Forward.

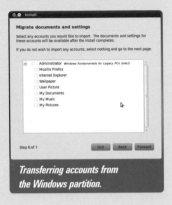

Transferring accounts from the Windows partition.

9 Confirmation

You're almost there – you just need to confirm that you're ready to go ahead:

Up until this point, nothing has been changed on your hard drive (unless you partitioned manually), so it's a final opportunity to check down the list on the screen and make sure that everything is going to happen as you intended. If you have second thoughts, you can click the Back button to go back to a previous step and make alterations.

There's an Advanced button here which you don't need to be concerned with now, but for future reference this lets you determine whether or not to install the boot loader (the program at the start of your hard drive that loads Linux and lets you choose between Linux and Windows if applicable), and set a proxy server for any downloads that the installer may wish to do.

When you're sure that you want to go ahead, click Install.

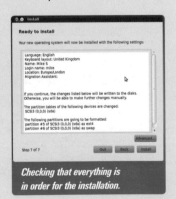

Checking that everything is in order for the installation.

10 Copying the files

Now the installer will do its work, first by partitioning the hard drive to make room for the new Linux installation:

Then it will copy the files onto your hard drive. Depending on the speed of your system, this could take a while, but the progress bar will give you a rough indication of how long it's going to take. Why not have a lovely cup of tea?

If your PC is connected to the Internet, the Ubuntu installer will also try to retrieve extra packages and updates – this isn't essential, though, so if your connection isn't very fast or you'd rather get on with the installation, click the Skip button.

Resizing a hard drive and formatting the new space.

11 Finish!

When the file copying is complete, you'll be prompted to restart the machine:

Hit Enter and your PC will shut down, ejecting the Ubuntu CD in the process (so that you don't boot up from it next time). After you've taken out the disc, hit Enter and the PC will restart, booting up into your new Linux installation.

The installation is done.

INSTALLATION
Rebooting and logging in

So that's it! The installation is complete. If you chose to log in automatically then you'll be straight at your new Linux desktop, which we'll explore in Section 2. Alternatively, if you didn't choose auto log-in then you'll see this screen first:

Logging in.

Click on your username and enter your password, and you'll be taken to the desktop. (Note that after clicking your username a panel of options will appear along the bottom of the screen – you don't need to change them now, but in future bear in mind that you can change your keyboard layout and language here. There's also a power button in the bottom-right corner that you can use to shut down without logging in first.)

You can shut down the computer directly from the login screen.

⚠ Where is windows?

What happened to Windows? If you installed a dual-boot system, keeping Windows intact, you'll be wondering how to access it again. Well, next time you reboot or start your machine, a menu like this should appear:

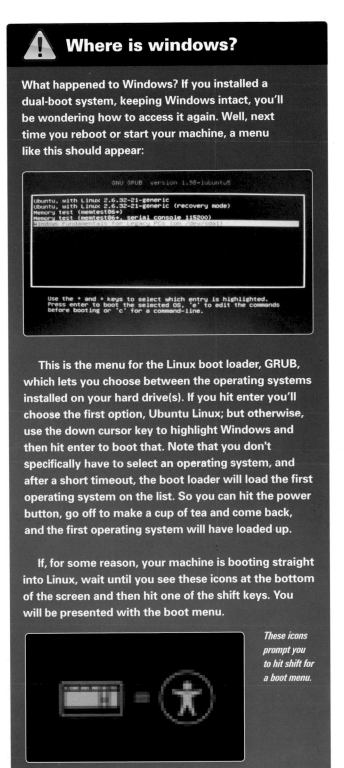

This is the menu for the Linux boot loader, GRUB, which lets you choose between the operating systems installed on your hard drive(s). If you hit enter you'll choose the first option, Ubuntu Linux; but otherwise, use the down cursor key to highlight Windows and then hit enter to boot that. Note that you don't specifically have to select an operating system, and after a short timeout, the boot loader will load the first operating system on the list. So you can hit the power button, go off to make a cup of tea and come back, and the first operating system will have loaded up.

If, for some reason, your machine is booting straight into Linux, wait until you see these icons at the bottom of the screen and then hit one of the shift keys. You will be presented with the boot menu.

These icons prompt you to hit shift for a boot menu.

INSTALLATION
Troubleshooting

If you had problems booting at the start of this section, and couldn't reach the installation stages, there are some things to try. Boot again from the CD and when you see these icons at the bottom of the screen:

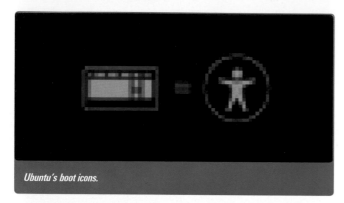

Ubuntu's boot icons.

Press one of the shift keys and you'll arrive at the disk's (normally hidden) boot menu:

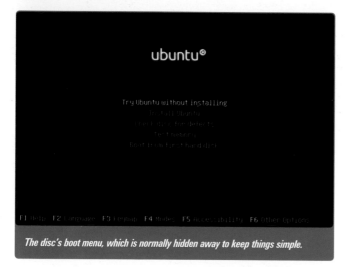

The disc's boot menu, which is normally hidden away to keep things simple.

If you suspect that there's a problem with the disc, use the cursor keys to select the 'Check disc for defects' option and hit Enter. If Ubuntu confirms that the disc is defective, contact Haynes for a replacement, or (if you're in a hurry) go to **www. ubuntu.com** where you can download the latest release.

Memory problems can manifest themselves in strange ways, with graphics corruption and random crashes, so another option worth trying in the boot menu is 'Test memory'. If Ubuntu appears to boot but then freezes at a certain stage, it might be having trouble detecting a certain

piece of hardware on your machine. It's a good idea to remove anything non-essential (such as scanners and printers) and then try installing again.

You can make Linux more tolerant of problematic hardware by hitting the F6 key at the CD boot menu, and hitting Enter to check various options in the menu that appears:

Use the cursor keys and Enter to select the first four (put crosses next to them), then press Escape to leave the menu and Enter to boot the machine. This will increase the chances of Linux booting – especially on older hardware – but if you still get stuck, see the Appendix for information on getting help online.

Editing boot options.

⚠ Hardware compatibility

There are literally millions of combinations of computer hardware out there, and it can be something of a minefield to make sure it all works correctly and in unison. Computer operating systems have an enormous job to accurately detect and configure such a vast range of hardware, and occasionally it doesn't work as smoothly as it should. For this reason we recommend unplugging unnecessary devices during the installation stage, so that the operating system doesn't get confused.

As Linux increases in popularity, more and more hardware manufacturers are starting to add Linux support and noting this on their product packaging. When you're out shopping for a new peripheral or component, keep an eye out for Linux support – although don't be disheartened if your favourite piece of kit doesn't advertise Linux on the box. Many devices are supported by the community and will work regardless.

INSTALLATION
Boot and install options

By far and away the best way to experience Linux is with a dedicated, full hard drive installation, as we've covered. However, you may remember that when the installer appeared, in the first screen there was a button marked Try Ubuntu. This runs the distribution in 'live' mode, that is, straight from the CD, without having to install anything. It won't touch anything on your hard drive.

We haven't covered this mode here because:

- It runs very slowly from the disc – much slower than from the hard drive.
- You can't save files as it has nowhere to store them (except for external media).
- As you've bought a book on Linux, you don't just plan to get your toes wet in the Linux pool but dive right in!

This mode can be useful, however, if you want to demonstrate the power of Linux on someone else's machine – you can take the disc over to a friend's PC,

boot it up and show them how great Linux is without having to repartition their hard drive. Another handy feature of live mode is the ability to test a PC's Linux compatibility. For instance, if you have your eye on a new PC at a local shop, but you're not sure how well it'll work with Linux, take the Linux CD along, boot it up and run it in live mode to get an idea of how well the graphics, sound, networking and so forth work. (Of course, it's a good idea to ask the shop owner first!)

⚠ Installing onto a partition

Meanwhile, if you access the Ubuntu CD in a file manager you'll see a Windows program called WUBI.EXE. This is a system that lets you install Linux inside a Windows partition, with the Linux filesystem being represented as a single file. As with live mode, this can be a useful way to demonstrate Linux to those who are very cautious about trying it, but it has a lot of limitations: it doesn't perform as well, hibernation mode isn't supported, and if you have any problems with the Windows installation then they affect the Ubuntu installation too. Consequently, for all serious Linux users we recommend the dedicated installation method as covered earlier; but if you want to demo the WUBI version on someone else's Windows machine then see http://wiki.ubuntu. com/WubiGuide for more information.

Looking to see how well Linux will work on a Windows box? Pop in the CD and go!

The desktop

02.

In this section

THE DESKTOP
Exploring the interface

Here it is, your brand new operating system in all its purple glory.

Ubuntu's graphical interface is a well-crafted mixture of long-standing GUI traditions and new features that you'll enjoy using. By default the desktop is completely bare, but, as we'll see in a moment, you can use it to hold files and program launchers. Pretty much everything on the desktop and in the various menus

is accessible by left-clicking with the mouse, but as with Windows, you can bring up more advanced options and contextual menus by right-clicking on an item. Whenever you come across an icon that's new to you, try hovering over it with the mouse to bring up an informational tooltip, or right-clicking. First off, though, let's divide the screen into four corners and see what each part does.

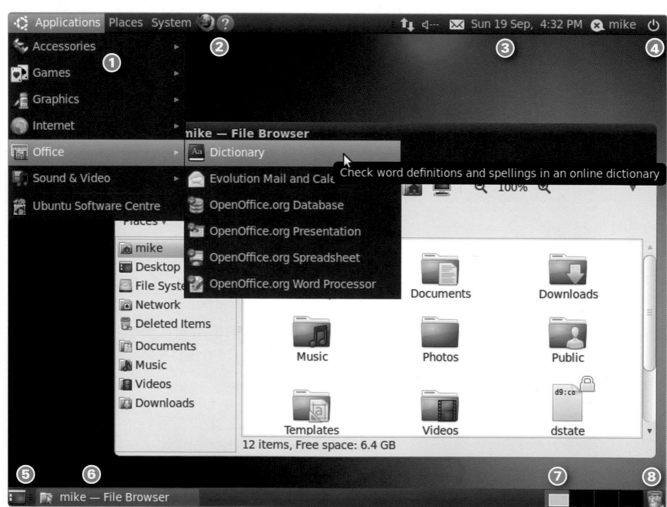

1. **Application menus**
2. **Quick program launchers**
3. **System tray**
4. **Log out/shutdown button**
5. **Show desktop button**
6. **Taskbar for running programs**
7. **Workspace switcher**
8. **Wastebasket**

1 Navigating menus

In the top-left corner are the desktop menus:

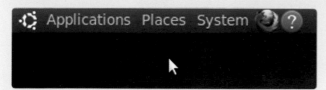

These always remain visible, no matter what program you're using, and are what you use to launch programs and browse your files. Click the Applications menu to open up a list of submenus containing the software installed on your system:

Essentially, this is similar to the Start menu in Windows. Software is organised by category, and at the bottom of the list you can see the Ubuntu Software Centre, a program to download more programs from the Internet – we'll cover that later. The next menu is Places:

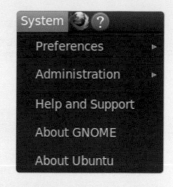

Meanwhile, the System menu provides access to settings and administration tools:

Inside the Preferences submenu you'll find utilities for changing the way you use the computer, such as keyboard short cuts, mouse settings, appearance settings and so forth, while in the Administration submenu you'll see more advanced tools for changing the workings of the system – hardware drivers, log file viewing, update management and more. Hover the mouse over an item in the list to see a tooltip with more information about what it does:

Many of the programs in the Administration submenu make changes to core system files, and therefore when you run them, you'll be asked for your password. This prevents other users from tampering with your machine, and also stops any program you download from the Internet from causing havoc. Without entering your password, you can only modify your personal files in your home folder, so the system is safe and secure.

This is what you use to open up the file manager. We'll cover file management in a moment, but the Home Folder is where all of your personal files are stored, and then there are Documents, Music, Pictures and other folders inside it. You can also click Computer to browse system files in your installation, and Connect to Server to retrieve files from another machine on your network (if applicable to your set-up).

2 Launching applications

To the right of the menus are program launchers:

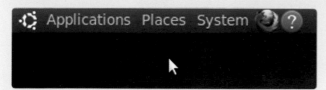

Hover the mouse pointer over them for a tooltip to see what they do – by default you have the Firefox web browser and access to the built-in help. It's handy to keep some of your most-used programs in this bunch of icons, so that you can access them without having to go through the menus: to do this, find the program you want in the Applications menu, then click and drag its icon into the panel next to the other icons. You can add as many icons as you like here (space permitting!), and to remove one right-click on it:

3 The system tray

Over in the top-right corner we have a collection of icons and snippets of text. The first three are part of a 'system tray', much like the collection of icons you see in the right-hand side of a Windows taskbar:

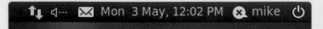

The first icon indicates the networking status, and its appearance may differ depending on the type of connection you have – ie whether it's wired or wireless. (For a guide to connecting to the Internet, see Section 3). Left-click on the icon to find out which connection it's using, and right-click to access the various properties for the connection.

The second icon is the volume control. Left-click it to bring up a slider to change the loudness of audio output, or choose Sound Preferences to have finer control over the various channels available on your sound card and the microphone volume.

Lastly in this trio of icons is the envelope. At the moment this doesn't do much, but as you set up email and instant messaging (as covered in Section 3) it will become active and let you know if there's something you need to be aware of, such as a new message in your Inbox.

After the system tray you have this:

First up is the date and time. You might not want to see all of this information on your screen – it takes up room if you're on a small display – in which case, right-click on the date and choose Preferences to bring up this dialog:

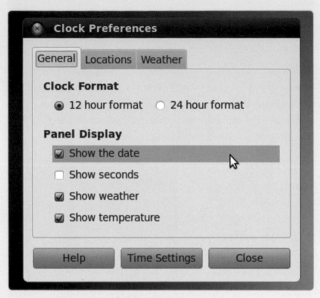

Here you can determine how much information is shown in the top-right panel, or click the Time Settings button at the bottom to set the date and time. Back in the panel, clicking on the speech bubble with your username next to it brings up this menu:

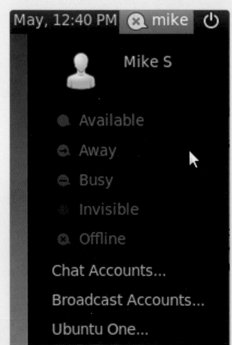

The user menu.

This is largely inactive at the moment, but when you run an instant messaging program (Section 3) you'll be able to change your status quickly here. If you left-click on your name at the top of this menu, a window will pop up that lets you customise your personal information:

Here you can click on the button at top left to change your icon, or alter your password with the Change Password button at top right.

Finally, the last thing in the top-right panel is the power button. As you'd expect, this is the button to hit when you want to shut down or restart the machine:

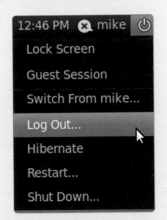

The bottom two options do exactly as they say, but it's also worth noting the Lock Screen and Guest Session choices. The first blanks your screen and then requires your password to reactivate it, so it's a useful facility if you're running Linux in a business setting, while Guest Session creates a temporary user account.

This is an excellent feature when someone else wants to use your machine but you don't want them to (accidentally or deliberately!) tamper with your files and settings. Activate the Guest Session, let them do what they want, then click the power button and Log Out to finish it.

If your PC supports it, you'll also see a Hibernate option: this puts the machine into a suspended state with little or no power usage. It's especially useful on laptops where you don't want to be booting up and shutting down every five minutes when you're on the move.

Where do deleted files go?

To the right of the desktop switcher boxes is the wastebasket, aka the trash can, recycle bin or other names that OS developers have given it down the years. It's very simple: if you delete a file, it will end up here first in case you want to retrieve it later. You can left-click on the wastebasket icon to see the contents, or right-click and choose 'Empty the Deleted Items folder' to permanently erase all files stored in it.

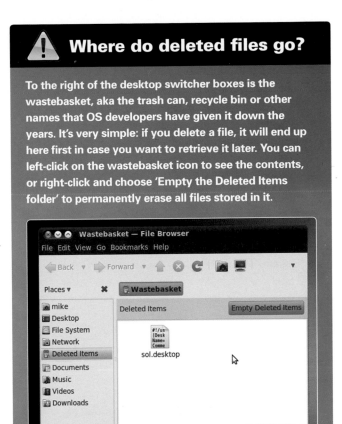

4 Exploring the bottom panels
Let's move down to the bottom-left corner:

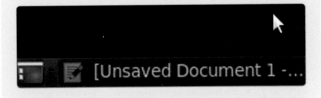

This contains the taskbar. If you open a program (eg Applications > Accessories > gEdit Text Editor from the top-left desktop menu), you'll see an entry for it appear in the taskbar. This is very much like the taskbar used in Windows: you can right-click on a button to perform actions on a window, such as maximising it or closing it. Note that when a window is minimised, its title is surrounded by square brackets in the taskbar.

To the far left is a small purple icon. Clicking this minimises all visible windows on the screen to the taskbar; clicking it again restores those windows. It's a handy button when you have multiple windows open and you need to quickly view or manipulate some files on the desktop.

5 Virtual desktops

However, minimising isn't the only way to cut down on window clutter. Looking at the bottom-right of the screen we see this:

For many years (and long before Windows and Mac OS X had this functionality), Linux has included virtual desktops. Each of the four boxes here is a standalone desktop that can contain its own set of applications. Try it out: launch a program (eg Applications > Accessories > gEdit) from the menu. Then click into another box, and you'll see that the text editor window disappears. Indeed, it's no longer even in the taskbar. Now launch another program (eg Applications > Accessories > Calculator), and click in the first desktop box to return back to where you were. You'll see that you can switch back and forth in the desktops using the boxes in the panel.

Effectively, virtual desktops multiply your working space and make it easy to have specialised desktops for certain applications. For instance, you could use the first desktop for running Internet software such as a browser and instant messenger, while in the second desktop you could have a set of serious office programs running.

Ubuntu includes four virtual desktops by default – if you find that too many, or you want even more, right-click on one of the boxes and choose Preferences from the pop-up menu that appears:

Here you can modify the number of workspaces (a synonym for virtual desktops), and even give them names.

6 Managing windows

Finally, let's have a look at window management. Open a program from the Applications menu and look at the titlebar:

On the left-hand side there are three buttons. In order, these are: close, minimise to the taskbar, and maximise (make full screen). When you maximise a window the third button will turn into a box – click it to return the window to its previous size. You can manually resize windows by clicking and dragging the edges, but the areas to grab these tend to be very small, so try the bottom-right corner instead. When the mouse pointer is over an area that can be used to resize a window, the cursor will change to a different shape like this:

If you want to move a window to a different virtual desktop, right-click on the titlebar and go into the Move to Another Workspace menu that appears:

The Linux desktop includes various keyboard short cuts for speeding up your work, making it less of a necessity to keep reaching over for the mouse when you're working. Here are the most important ones to know:

- **Alt+F4 – Close window.**
- **Alt+F10 – Maximise window.**
- **Alt+F9 – Minimise window.**
- **Alt+F1 – Open the Applications menu (use the cursor keys and Enter to navigate through and launch programs).**
- **Ctrl+Alt+d – Minimise all applications and show the desktop.**
- **Ctrl+Alt+l – Lock the screen (requiring your password to go back to the desktop).**
- **Ctrl+Alt+left cursor – Switch to a virtual desktop to the left.**
- **Ctrl+Alt+right cursor – Switch to a virtual desktop to the right.**

You can alter these and create more by going to System > Preferences > Keyboard Shortcuts in the desktop menu.

THE DESKTOP
Nautilus file manager

ile management is one of those topics that is inevitably rather dull, but still, it's something we all have to do. Your Linux installation is equipped with a very powerful file manager called Nautilus that lets you browse remote hard drives over the network as if they were connected to your own machine, but to start with let's concentrate on the basics.

1 Launching Nautilus
You can launch Nautilus by clicking Places > Home Folder in the desktop menu:

In terms of the interface, it's very much what you'd expect in a file manager: there's a list of commonly accessed drives and locations down the left-hand side, while the right-hand panel contains your files and folders. Your home folder (aka home directory) is the place where you store your personal files, somewhat like My Documents in the Windows world, and its location is in /home/username (replace username with your actual username) on the hard drive. (We cover the layout of the Linux filesystem in more detail in Section 6.)

By default Ubuntu creates a bunch of folders for your music, documents, pictures and so forth, while there's a dedicated downloads folder for files that you retrieve from the web. Double-click a folder to access its contents. The Desktop folder shows you the same view as the files on your desktop – right now it's empty, though. As you're navigating, use the back and forward buttons in the toolbar at the top of the window to switch between the folder you've just visited, and the up arrow button to step up a level in the directory hierarchy.

2 Manipulating files
To make a new folder, just right-click in the file manager window and choose Create Folder:

It will appear in the window and you can type in a name for it.

Moving files and folders around is simple: click and drag them to drop them into another folder. You can even go to Places

> Home Folder again to open up another file manager window, and drag and drop files between the two windows. When you click and drag a file, as you hover it over a folder you'll see that a small arrow appears; this means that the file is going to be moved. If you'd like to copy the file instead, ie make a new version of it in the directory, hold down the Ctrl key while dragging and you'll see that the arrow changes into a plus sign.

⚠ Selecting multiple files

To select multiple items at once, click and drag in a blank area to draw a box around the files that you want to select:

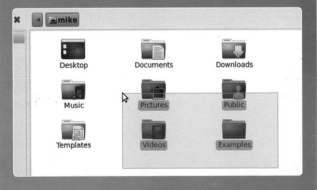

You can then click and drag one of the selected files to move or copy them all at once.

3 File options

Let's look at the options available when you right-click on a file. A menu like this will appear, although the contents of the menu will vary depending on the file type:

To get rid of the file, choose 'Move to the Deleted Items folder'. This will put it in the wastebasket in the bottom-right corner, as covered before. (A quick tip: if you want to delete a file immediately without moving it through the wastebasket first, click to select it and then press Shift+Delete.)

At the top of the right-click list you'll see some 'Open with' options – these show the programs that are associated with this type of file. If you know that you want to view or edit the file in a different program, choose the Open with Other Application option:

In the dialog box that appears, you'll see a complete list of all of the programs installed on your system that can work with this particular type of file.

Back in the right-click menu, there are some other options worth looking at. You can rename the file or stretch its icon to make it look bigger in the file manager, or you can compress it to save room on your drive:

When compressing a file or folder, it's important to choose the right format in the drop-down box to the right of the filename. .tar.gz is the most common type of compressed archive on Linux, and .tar.bz2 is a similar format that squeezes files down to even smaller sizes (albeit taking a bit more time to do so), but if you're going to be sharing an archive with a Windows machine, .zip is the better choice – it's well supported on that platform.

The final option in the right-click menu is Properties. This brings up a dialog box providing lots of information about the file or folder:

You can see its size, the exact location on the disk, and when it was last accessed (viewed) and modified. By clicking the Emblems tab you can assign small pictures to go alongside the file's icon, and under Permissions you can determine whether other users on the system can modify the file:

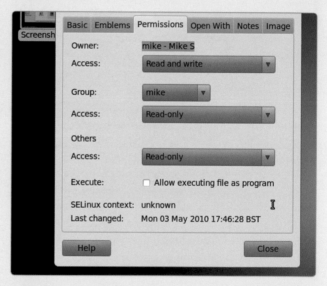

(User management and privileges is covered in Section 6.) An important option to note here is the 'Execute' checkbox: if you select this, you will be able to run a file by double-clicking it. To err on the safe side, Linux doesn't let you execute files without explicitly checking this box, so that you don't accidentally end up running nasty scripts from the Internet. However, if you do download a file that you're absolutely sure you need to run (eg a game installer that ends in .bin) then access the properties for the file, check this box, and then double-click the file to run it.

4 Getting files from the network

If there are other accessible computers on your local network, click Places > Network from the desktop menu to view them. To connect to a specific machine, click Places > Connect to Server:

In the drop-down list at the top you can choose from a range of protocols – Windows shares, FTP servers, SSH servers and more. Enter the details for the machine and click Connect:

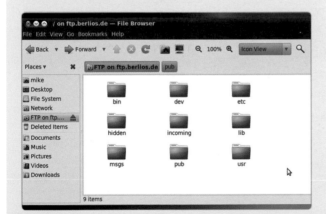

All being well, you can now browse the server and (if you have the right permissions) transfer files to and from it, as if it were a hard drive on your local machine. When you're done, click the eject button next to the server name in the left-hand panel of the file manager.

5 External drives

Accessing external USB drives is easy: just plug it in and a new file manager window will appear, showing the contents of the device. You will also find an icon for it on the desktop, and via Places > Computer. As with other operating systems, it's not a good idea to remove a device straight after you've copied files on to it – even if the copying operation appears to be complete, the operating system's disk buffers may still contain data to be written. Right-click on the icon for the drive and choose Safely Remove Device, and this will ensure that the data on the drive doesn't get corrupted. You can then remove it from the USB port.

Also in Places > Computer you'll find icons for other drives or partitions in your machine. If you simply have a single hard drive that's entirely dedicated to Linux, you'll only see one icon here, File System. However, if you have Windows on another partition on the disk (or on another drive) then you will be able to access the contents of it here.

⚠ Adding items to the desktop

As mentioned earlier, the desktop is rather plain in its default state. You can drag files from the file manager on to the desktop if you need to access them regularly, but the desktop can also hold program launchers too.

Open up the Applications menu and locate the program that you want to put on the desktop, then left-click and drag its icon to an empty space on the desktop. To get rid of the icon, just click on it once to select it and press the Delete button on your keyboard. (This won't delete the program itself – just the launcher icon.)

THE DESKTOP
The included software

Ubuntu Linux is supplied with an excellent collection of software that covers the vast majority of day-to-day tasks. If you've come from a Windows background you'll be very happy to see that you have large (and normally very costly) pieces of software such as an office suite included for free. Indeed, every program available in the menus is free, open source and developed by communities of passionate developers. It's a testament to what can be achieved when people work together.

Let's have a look at some of the programs that are included. We're going to explore many of these in greater depth later on in this book, showing you how to make use of the many features they include, but here we'll have a quick run-through to help you get your bearings. Firstly, click Applications and go into the Accessories menu:

Calculator

A simple desktop calculator, and very handy to have around. Well, it looks very simple the first time you start it, but there's a much greater range of functionality hidden under the hood. Click into the View menu and you can choose different layouts with more buttons and features. There's a scientific mode, a financial mode, and even a programmer's mode that lets you play around with binary arithmetic.

Character map

This tiny utility comes in useful if you need to input a character that's not on your keyboard. It's especially good for finding characters in foreign writing systems.

Disk Usage Analyser

When you're transferring large videos from a digital camera or downloading Linux ISOs off the Internet, it's all too easy to run low on disk space without knowing it. This utility gives you a quick, at-a-glance look at the status of your drives, so you can see if it's time to get concerned and start clearing out old files.

gEdit Text Editor

In many respects, this text editing utility is similar to Notepad on Windows, but it includes a lot more functionality. For starters, it has syntax highlighting (coloured keywords) for a wide variety of programming languages, and also a hugely powerful plugins system that lets you expand the editor with add-on features (click Edit > Preferences and then the Plugins tab). There's also a spelling checker that you can find under the Tools menu.

Search for Files

No prizes for guessing that this locates files on your system. Type in the name of the file you're looking for (or a few letters to match multiple files) and hit Enter. By default this tool only searches in your home folder; if you want to find files elsewhere on the computer, click the 'Look in folder' drop-down list and choose File System.

Terminal

This opens up the command line window. For most tasks you'll never need to touch the command line, but if you want to explore further in Linux then command line knowledge comes in very useful. You'll find a detailed guide to the command line in Section 7.

Tomboy Notes

You could use the gEdit text editor for tapping down quick notes, but Tomboy is a lot more versatile, letting you create multiple windows of notes and linking between them. Click the Text button on the toolbar to add formatting to parts of the note, and right-click on a note for more options. When you start Tomboy, a new note-like icon will appear in the system tray at the top of the screen – left-click it to create new note windows.

Next up is the Games submenu:

AisleRiot Solitaire

No operating system would be complete without a bunch of card games, and Ubuntu Linux doesn't disappoint. AisleRiot wipes the floor with the competition by offering a vast range of card game types in a single application: click Game > Select Game from the menu and you'll see a long, scrollable list with all the different variants available.

gbrainy

Brain-training games have been all the rage since the Nintendo DS appeared, and Ubuntu has its own offering here. There are mini-games to test your logic, memory and calculation skills.

Mahjongg

This isn't Mahjongg as in the proper, four-player tile-slamming capers from the Far East, but a simplified game in which you click tiles to match them. It's not particularly demanding but still a good way to relax.

Mines

A clone of the hugely popular Minesweeper game. Click blocks to see how many mines are surrounding them, but if you accidentally click on a mine block, it's game over. If the standard game is too easy for you, click Settings > Preferences in the menu to choose larger playing areas.

Quadrapassel

This is Tetris. Good old-fashioned Tetris. Blocks fall from the top of the screen; use the cursor keys to move them left and right, and press up to rotate them. The goal is to fill the well at the bottom of the screen with complete lines, which then disappear. If you leave gaps, the pieces will keep stacking up – and if they reach the top of the screen, it's game over. Hint: press the space bar to immediately drop a piece to the bottom. Hint 2: this really is one of the most addictive games in the history of existence.

Sudoku

Lastly, there's an implementation of the maths game that has taken the world by storm in recent years.

It's deceptively simple: enter numbers into blank boxes so that there is only one of that number in the 3x3 grid, and only one of that number in the horizontal and vertical lines that it's on. It sounds easy at first, but can be devilishly difficult.

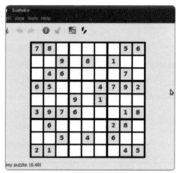

Moving on to the Graphics submenu:

F-Spot Photo Manager

This program lets you import images from your digital camera (or a folder on your hard drive), edit them (change size, rotate etc) and then export them to an online photo gallery. It's covered in detail in Section 5.

OpenOffice.org Drawing

Part of the OpenOffice.org suite, this is a vector graphics editor. Click the buttons along the bottom to draw shapes, lines and icons, and the toolbar near the top to change colour and line width settings. When you're done, use the File menu at the top to save your work.

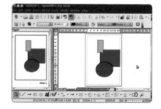

Simple Scan

If you have a scanner connected to your machine, use this utility to grab pictures from it. When it starts up, it will try to detect your scanner, and then you can click the Scan button in the top-left to begin the process. If you're happy with the results, click the Save button to store the resulting image.

Now on to the Internet submenu:

Empathy IM Client
This is a powerful instant messaging program that works with a wide variety of chat protocols (AIM, MSN, Google Talk etc). It's covered in detail in Section 3.

Firefox Web Browser
The second most popular browser in the world, and deservedly so. Firefox is fast, secure and there are thousands of extensions available to make it even better.

Gwibber Social Client
If you're a regular user of social networking tools, this is well worth investigating. It lets you communicate on Twitter, Facebook, Flickr and other services from a single app, without having to navigate around lots of web pages. When you start it up you'll be prompted to select the social networking service that you want, and then enter your login details.

Remote Desktop Viewer
As a new Linux user, you won't need this right now, but it's worth knowing that it exists for the future. This lets you connect to other machines and operate them as if you were sitting directly in front of them. Essentially, the remote machine's display is transmitted over the network – like a TV signal – and then your mouse and keyboard movements are sent back to that machine. It's useful for supporting other Linux users over the Internet and fixing problems for them.

Transmission BitTorrent Client
This program downloads files from BitTorrent, the peer-to-peer (P2P) file-sharing network. See Section 3 for a detailed usage guide.

Under the Office menu:

Dictionary
A simple little utility that looks up the definition of words:

Evolution
A robust mail client and calendaring tool that's covered in depth in Section 3, along with the word processor, spreadsheet and presentation components of the OpenOffice.org office suite, each of which are explored in Section 4.

The final submenu is Sound & Video:

Brasero Disc Burner
This program lets you write data to CD-Rs and DVD-Rs, be it audio, video or plain files for backup purposes. It's covered in Section 5.

Movie Player
Also known as Totem, this lets you view video files. See Section 5 for more.

PiTiVi Video Editor
If you want to splice together some home movies, with extra soundtracks and effects, look here. It balances a decent set of features with being easy to get started with and use.

Rhythmbox Music Player
This isn't just a simple audio player, but a complete music collection manager that lets you sort tracks into playlists and import files from MP3 players such as iPods. See Section 5 for a guide.

Sound Recorder
Another small utility that no modern operating system can be without. Plug in your microphone, hit the red circle button on the toolbar and start talking. By default it will save audio files in Ogg format, a free format that's popular in the Linux world, but if you're going to be sharing files with Windows users we recommend opting for the .wav format.

THE DESKTOP
Downloading programs

As we've seen, this is a great range of software to have out-of-the-box, and the programs included with Ubuntu demonstrate some of the best technology in the free software world. However, it is only a small fraction of what's available, and you can explore a much wider selection of applications via the Internet. But you don't have to spend hours trawling through websites, clicking on links and hoping that the files are still there – Ubuntu includes a very powerful software installation system that grabs what you need from the Internet with a few mouse clicks.

1 Starting the Software Centre

Go to Applications > Ubuntu Software Centre in the main desktop menu:

2 Exploring the interface

When it starts up you'll see this screen:

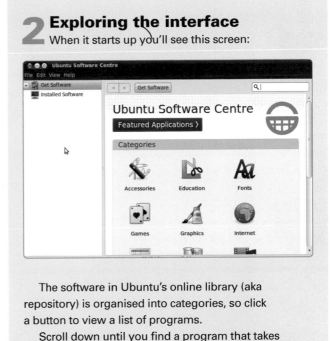

The software in Ubuntu's online library (aka repository) is organised into categories, so click a button to view a list of programs.

Scroll down until you find a program that takes your interest, and then click on the More Info button inside its entry in the list. You'll see a screen similar to this, providing a detailed description of the program along with a screenshot and a link to its website:

3 Installing the app

If you want this program, click the Install button at the top of the description. You may be asked for your password as a security measure, because you're about to install new files on to the system. Then you'll see a progress bar showing how much of the download has been completed:

Small utilities will only take a minute or two on a regular broadband connection; large applications could take up to an hour. Still, nothing stops you from browsing other software at the same time!

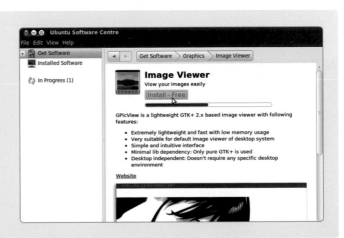

Selected software

Here are some of the best free Linux applications that aren't included in Ubuntu but are very well worth trying out – you can locate them using the search box in the top-right corner of the Software Centre. (Make sure that you're searching the entire software collection and not just a specific category by clicking Get Software towards the top first.)

Gimp

The GNU Image Manipulation Program. This is a tremendously powerful image editor – indeed, it used to be part of Ubuntu but was deemed too powerful for most users and replaced with F-Spot instead! However, if you find F-Spot too limiting and want to have more control over your images, install this. It's supplied with an impressive array of filters, and generally provides all of the important functionality of Adobe Photoshop at zero cost.

Scribus

A desktop publishing (DTP) application. For small jobs such as letters and local newsletters, the word processor in OpenOffice.org does a more than adequate job, but if you're looking for something that places greater emphasis on layout and page design, this is the program you need.

AbiWord

A fast and lightweight word processor. It doesn't have all the power-user features of OpenOffice.org Writer, but if you're looking for something a bit zippier (especially for older machines) then this is a great choice.

Inkscape

For vector graphics editing, Inkscape is the leading program on Linux. It's similar to Adobe Illustrator and CorelDraw, but uses the web standard SVG (Scalable Vector Graphics) format and has many advanced features such as alpha blending, markers and complex path operations.

Gnumeric

This spreadsheet program is, like AbiWord, a light alternative to the larger office suite. It can read Microsoft Excel documents.

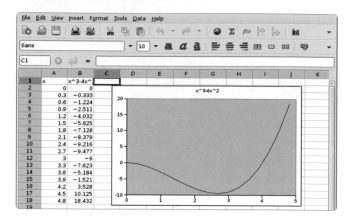

Gramps

Genealogy software. Thanks to the Internet it's becoming ever easier to track down distant relatives and construct family trees, and with Gramps you can organise names, places and other facts. It's the leading piece of genealogy software on Linux and stacks up very well against the commercial competition.

GnuCash

This is the best personal finance suite available on Linux, keeping track of your incoming and outgoing cashflows. If you're buried under a pile of bills and invoices and you're finding it hard to keep track of everything, take this for a test run.

MyPaint

While you have F-Spot for touching up photos and Gimp for advanced image manipulation, MyPaint provides a simple, no-frills drawing program, much like the Paint program included with Windows. It's useful for making quick sketches, and if you have children they'll enjoy playing around with it too.

X-Chat

IRC (Internet Relay Chat) doesn't get as much attention as instant messaging, but it's still commonly used, especially among free software developers. This program lets you create a nickname, join an IRC network and begin chatting with other users.

GCompris

There is even something to keep the children busy. GCompris is a suite of educational programs, covering maths, reading, memory practice, telling the time, keyboard skills and various other subjects. It's colourful, cheerful and fun.

VirtualBox

An exceptionally valuable piece of software that emulates a complete PC on your desktop. Its hard drive is emulated as a file on your machine, and you can use it to install Windows (or other Linux distributions) without having to reboot your machine. If you need Windows for the occasional program but you don't want the hassle of endlessly restarting your machine, install this.

Audacity

The Sound Recorder utility included with Ubuntu is a very basic and limited tool. For a more advanced sound file editor, try Audacity, which lets you piece together multiple tracks, chop sections out of a file, apply filters and save the results in various formats. It's a great tool for converting old cassette tape and vinyl recordings into digital format.

Neverball

A highly polished and very entertaining 3D game in which you manipulate a playing area with the mouse to roll a ball around on it. It requires careful mouse control and nerves of steel at times . . . which makes it all the more fun!

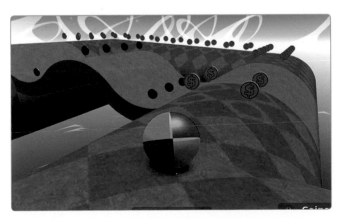

Command line programs?

Note that while many applications in the library run in GUI mode (ie they have a graphical user interface), some of them – especially development tools and server software – only operate at the command line in text mode. If you've installed a graphical program, you will be able to find it in one of the submenus of the Applications menu, based on its category. For command line programs, open a terminal window and type the name of the program (in lower case), and that should give you an indication of what it does.

Freeciv

If you're looking for something more cerebral, this is a strategy game based on the classic Civilization. You work through the early years of human civilisation, enhancing your technologies and trying to take over the other peoples of the world.

LMMS

If you're looking to make music on your Linux machine, LMMS (the Linux MultiMedia Studio) deserves a close look. It's a free alternative to the likes of FL Studio Logic and Cubase, with a beat editor, piano roll, FX mixer and many effect plugins.

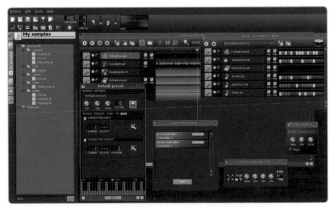

THE DESKTOP
Desktop appearance

If you've ever seen Ubuntu screenshots from older releases, you'll have noticed that they're always a rather unusual shade of browny-orange. With version 10.04, as included on the disk with this book, the Ubuntu team radically overhauled the interface and gave it the more striking black and purple colours that you see now. If they don't appeal to you, however, or you'd just like a change of scenery, then here's how to customise the look of your desktop.

1 Get a new background

First, right-click on a blank area of the desktop and choose Change Desktop Background. This window will appear, showing you the selection of images included with Ubuntu:

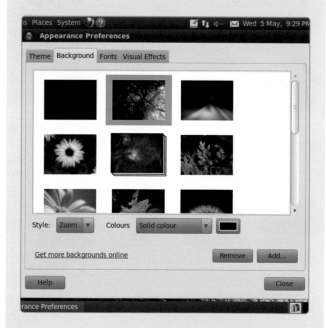

Click a picture and the background will change immediately. If you'd rather use one of your own pictures, click the Add button in the bottom-right corner and browse to the image on your hard drive. Some pictures have ratios and dimensions that may not match your particular monitor, so click the drop-down list next to Style to determine whether the picture should be zoomed, centred, stretched and so forth.

2 Try a new theme

To alter the theme of the desktop – that is, the colours and styles used for buttons, titlebars and menus – click System > Preferences > Appearance from the desktop menu to bring up this:

Click on an image to activate a theme:

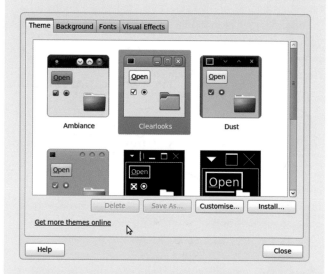

Some of the themes, such as those marked High Contrast, are not designed to look pretty on your desktop but rather to make the screen more visible for those with limited vision. Each theme is a collection of styles for the widgets (buttons), titlebars and other features of the desktop – but if you want to fine-tune each part individually, click the Customise button:

In this screen you can choose the exact style you want for buttons and window decorations, along with the colour scheme you want to use and even the look of the mouse pointer.

3 Get new themes online

Back in the main Appearance Preferences window, there's a link in the bottom-left corner titled 'Get more themes online'. If you're connected to the Internet and you click this, you'll be taken to a website where you can browse a collection of themes that other Linux users in the community have developed. Choose Controls and you can view themes that affect the buttons, menus and other widgets:

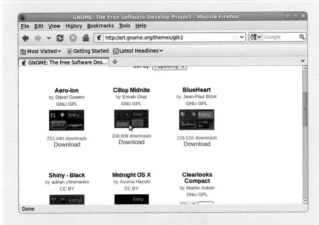

When you see one that you like, click the Download button and you'll be prompted to install the file in the Theme Installer like this:

Click OK and, when the theme is installed, the Appearance Preferences dialog will pop up again and ask you if you want to apply the new theme straight away. If you choose to, the look of your interface will change accordingly:

⚠ Linux and accessibility

As you've seen in step 2, it's easy to choose a desktop theme that's more suitable for those with vision impairments. You can customise font sizes to make them larger, and create a working environment much more suited for those with sight difficulties. Additionally, Linux includes other tools for those with disabilities, and you can find them by going to the System menu, then Preferences and Assistive Technologies.

In the keyboard settings, you'll see an option to turn on 'Sticky Keys', which is very useful for those who only have control of one arm. When you need to do a multi-key task, such as Alt+F4, with Sticky Keys you can press Alt on its own, and then F4 afterwards (instead of at the same time). Under the mouse options you can make the mouse auto-click when movement stops, which is not only a great aid for those with limitations but helps to combat RSI for everyone too.

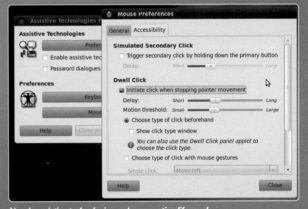

Linux's assistive technologies make computing life much easier for those with disabilities.

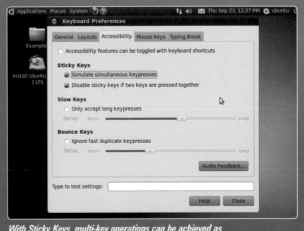

With Sticky Keys, multi-key operations can be achieved as a sequence of individual key presses.

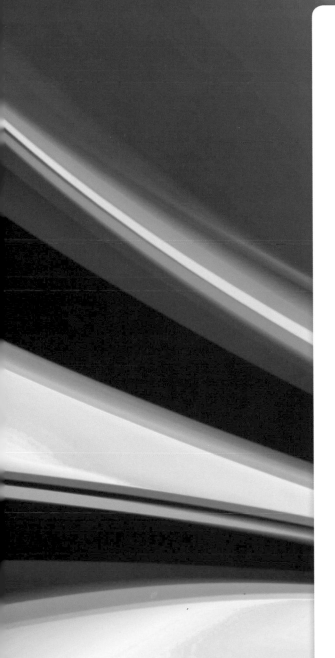

03.

The Internet

In this section

THE INTERNET
Connecting to the Internet

Linux tries to make the job of connecting to the Internet as seamless as possible: plug in a network cable and you're on your way. However, with the increasing use of wireless networking and a wide variety of Internet modems and routers available, you may have to perform some configuration beforehand. We'll cover the various options here.

1 Check your devices

Firstly: hardware. In a home setting, chances are that you have a broadband ADSL modem or router, usually supplied by your ISP (Internet services provider). Combined ADSL modem and routers with Ethernet ports are the simplest solution here. With these devices, all of the work of connecting to the Internet is handled on the router itself, so all you need is an Ethernet patch cable to connect your PC to the router and it will work straight away. Most routers use a web-based interface for accessing the settings and options – the documentation will give you the address, but normally you hook up the cable and enter something like http://10.0.0.138 into your browser's address bar.

An Ethernet (aka RJ45) connector.

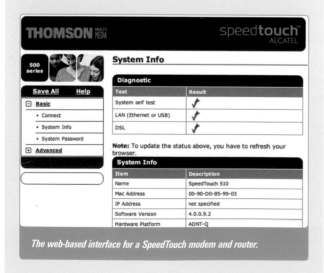

The web-based interface for a SpeedTouch modem and router.

2 Using the interface

In the web-based interface you can control the connection and set up advanced options such as port forwarding. Meanwhile, if you have a combined modem-router that functions as a WiFi access point, and you've installed Ubuntu on a PC that has a wireless card, you can try scanning for it. In the system tray at the top-right of the screen, left-click on the 'radar' icon and you'll bring up a menu, like this:

You'll see a list of available networks and their signal strengths. Networks with a padlock on the icon are secured, so if you try to connect you'll be prompted to supply a password.

3 Connecting to a hidden network

If you can't see your network on the list, try the 'Connect to Hidden Wireless Network' option, and if you still have no luck, right-click on the radar icon and make sure that the Enable Networking and Enable Wireless boxes are checked.

Configuring connections

To configure wired and wireless connections in detail, open the connection manager. This is accessed by right-clicking on the radar icon for wireless connections, or if you're using wired Ethernet, right-click on the up and down white arrows in the system tray. In either case, choose Edit Connections, and you'll see this window:

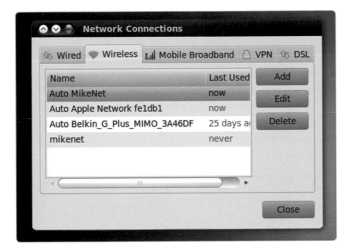

Along the top you can see tabs for different types of connections. In the Wireless tab, for instance, we can see the wireless access points that we've recently connected to (or tried to access). Click on one and then Edit to configure the connection like so:

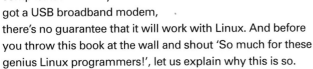

Here you can fine-tune security settings and choose whether or not to connect to this network automatically.

You'll notice the other tabs in the connection manager for Mobile Broadband and DSL. Things can get a bit more complicated here. If you've got a USB broadband modem, there's no guarantee that it will work with Linux. And before you throw this book at the wall and shout 'So much for these genius Linux programmers!', let us explain why this is so.

If you have a USB modem . . .

With standalone Ethernet/WiFi modem-router devices, as covered before, all of the Internet technology is inside the box. It instigates and manages all aspects of the connection, handling Internet data packets and so forth. Your Linux box is merely something that can tag on to that connection now – as indeed any computer with a TCP/IP Internet stack can.

With USB broadband modems, much of the hard work is shifted on to the CPU of the computer itself. They're not standalone Internet devices. Consequently, they need specific drivers to operate, and many Internet service providers are too ingrained in the Windows mentality to support alternative operating systems. The Linux community is working hard to create drivers based on scraps of information and specifications thrown out by the hardware vendors, but it's not easy.

Consequently, with USB modems and USB mobile broadband devices, all you can do is plug in the device, cross your fingers and hope that it works. If you're lucky, it'll be detected and set up automatically, and a pop-up status box will let you know. If you're not so lucky, right-click the network icon in the system tray and choose Edit Connections to bring up the connection manager as covered before, and see if you can find your device.

If you're still out of luck, telephone your ISP and ask them if they support Linux. You might be able to persuade them to swap your Windows-only USB modem with an OS-independent modem-router – perhaps for a little extra cost. If they're not cooperative, make it clear that you'll switch to an ISP that does provide Linux-compatible hardware! If you love your ISP and need to replace your device yourself, it's not tremendously costly. For instance, as of mid-2010 a ZyXEL Prestige 660R-D1 ADSL modem-router was available for £25 (USD $38). Whatever device you choose, make sure that: (A) It's an ADSL modem; (B) it also functions as a router; and (C) you connect to it via Ethernet. Then you should have no problems at all.

Connection information

Lastly, back to the up-and-running connection. To find out information about the connection, such as the MAC (hardware) address, connection speed and IP address that your computer has, right-click on the system tray connection icon (the radar or up–down arrows) and choose Connection Information:

Note that the IP address here is that of your machine on the local network, and not the IP address that you have on the Internet – to determine that, visit www.whatismyip.com.

THE INTERNET
The Firefox browser

Firefox is the second most popular web browser on the planet, and one of the most championed open-source projects of all time. In the early 2000s, with Netscape effectively destroyed by Microsoft's dominance, it looked like Internet Explorer was going to remain unchallenged for many years to come. Indeed it did, but with little serious competition in the market it soon became a stagnant mess of code, littered with bugs and security holes.

In the meantime, Netscape was open-sourced and became Mozilla, a popular-in-geek-circles browsing suite that was more standards-compliant than Internet Explorer but with demanding memory requirements. A bunch of programmers forked the project into the svelte and lean Firefox, built up a huge word-of-mouth campaign, and managed to take a big chunk away from Microsoft's browser. It also forced Microsoft to put more development effort into Internet Explorer. In the end, it was a result for everybody.

You may have already used Firefox on Windows or Mac OS X, in which case the next few paragraphs explaining the interface won't be hugely revealing, but in a moment we'll look at the more advanced features of the browser – short cuts, hidden settings and add-ons.

1 Launching the browser

To start Firefox, click Applications > Internet > Firefox Web Browser in the desktop menu, or alternatively the blue and orange icon on the top panel.

Then Firefox's main window will appear, with a customised home screen for searching the web and getting links to Ubuntu help. There's nothing especially surprising here: it looks and feels like a web browser.

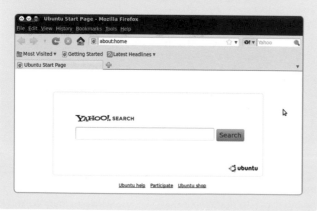

2 Exploring the toolbar

Along the top, beneath the menu, you have the main toolbar:

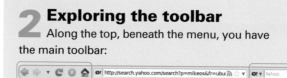

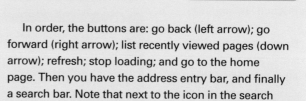

In order, the buttons are: go back (left arrow); go forward (right arrow); list recently viewed pages (down arrow); refresh; stop loading; and go to the home page. Then you have the address entry bar, and finally a search bar. Note that next to the icon in the search bar is a small arrow – if you click it you can change the search engine to something different:

3 Working with bookmarks

You'll notice that in the address bar, on the right-hand side, there's a faded-out star. By clicking this star you can instantly add the current web page to your bookmarks, via Bookmarks > Recently Bookmarked in the menu. This one-click star system lets you bookmark a bunch of pages in quick succession, eg if you're doing some research, without having to manually add lots of information. However, if you want to customise the information associated with the bookmark, click the star again:

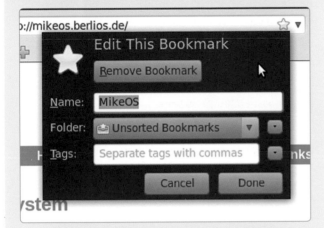

For more advanced bookmark management, click Bookmarks > Organize Bookmarks and a window will pop up in which you can right-click bookmark entries to remove them and drag them around between different folders:

Back to the browser: beneath the navigation toolbar is a bookmarks toolbar; click Most Visited to view a list of your most popular sites. If you want to remove this bar to save space, go to View > Toolbars in the menu and make sure that the box next to Bookmarks Toolbar is unchecked.

4 Mastering the tab bar

Then there's the tab bar. Firefox makes heavy use of tabbed browsing, so that you don't need to have lots of windows running. Middle-clicking on a link opens it in a new tab, which is a hugely useful short cut: you can skim over a list of search results, middle-clicking on the links you like and those pages will load in the background as you carry on searching. When you're done, you can then view those pages without having to wait for them to load.

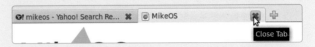

Click the 'x' buttons on tabs to close them, and the green plus sign to the right of the tabs to open a new, blank one.

Keyboard shortcuts

So, you can navigate the web, manage bookmarks and handle tabs – we've got the core elements of browsing covered. Before we move on to some more advanced features of Firefox, here are some cunning short cuts to save you time:

- **Ctrl+t – Open a new tab.**
- **Ctrl+w – Close the current tab, or if it's the last tab, close the window.**
- **Ctrl+l – Shift the focus to the address bar, so you can start typing in an address.**
- **Ctrl+k – Shift the focus to the web search bar.**
- **Tab – Move the focus to the next element in a page. This is hugely useful when you're entering information into a form, as you can hit tab to move between the boxes without reaching over for the mouse.**
- **Alt+Left cursor key – Go to the previous page in your history.**
- **Alt+Right cursor key – Go to the next page in your history.**
- **Ctrl++ (that's Ctrl with the plus key) – Zoom in.**
- **Ctrl+- (that's Ctrl with the minus key) – Zoom out.**
- **Ctrl+u – View page source.**
- **F5 – Reload page text.**
- **Shift+F5 – Reload entire page, including cached images.**
- **F11 – Switch to full screen mode. Press F11 to escape out of it.**

Over time you'll find that these save a huge amount of mousing around on the screen. You'll find yourself hitting Ctrl+t to open a new tab, followed by Ctrl+k to enter a search term, as if your fingers were operating automatically!

Adding new plugins

Let's move on to plugins. Firefox is a very capable browser, but there are a few things it doesn't do out of the box, and one is to support the Adobe Flash format. If you don't know what Flash is or you've got no reason to use it, lucky you – it's a closed, binary plugin that has a well-deserved reputation for eating up CPU cycles and slowing things down. But in fairness to Adobe, they are working on it all the time so it may perform better as you read this. Still, many video and games websites use it, so you probably can't escape from it.

1 Launching the browser

To install Flash, visit a website that requires Flash to be installed. You'll see a black bar beneath the tab bar like this:

However, don't be tempted to click the Install Missing Plugins button – this is something that is better achieved through Ubuntu's own software installation system.

2 Locate the software

Click Applications > Ubuntu Software Centre from the main desktop menu and use the search box in the top-right to search for 'flash':

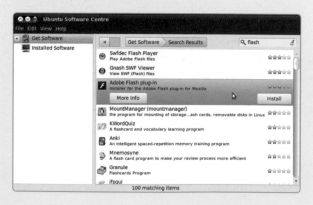

3 Install it!

Click on the entry for the Adobe Flash plugin and then click Install. You may be prompted for your password. Close the Software Centre and restart Firefox; then go back to the page that didn't work properly before. You will now see it in all its Flash-based glory:

Aside from Flash there are some lesser-known plugins that you may come across. If a page prompts you for one, try the Install Missing Plugins button in Firefox this time – it works with most plugins, but there can be occasional problems with Flash using that method, which is why we installed it via the Software Centre.

⚠ Begone, pop-up windows

Firefox tries to make your browsing experience as pleasant as possible, by removing some of the annoyances that plagued other browsers for years. For instance, it's extremely good at blocking pop-up windows, that perennial source of irritation on the web.

As with the plugins scenario, a black bar will appear beneath the tab bar, but this time it will tell you how many pop-up windows it has blocked. Now, in most cases this is great – pop-up windows are usually horrifically irksome adverts that make you want to punch the screen. However, some sites make legitimate use of pop-up windows so if you want to permit them for a particular site, click the Preferences button in the black bar and choose the 'Allow' option:

If you need to let pop-ups through for a particular site, it only takes one click.

Form data and your privacy

Another way in which Firefox tries to streamline your browsing is by saving form data: in other words, when you enter a username and password into a site, Firefox will offer to save it for you:

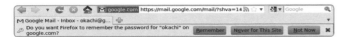

Click Remember to store your login details in Firefox's configuration files, or Never for This Site if it's an important account and you'd rather stay on the safe side, entering your details each time. If you're not sure and just want to get on with the job, click Not Now.

How can you manage the data that's stored? The solution is through Firefox's settings.

1 Open the Preferences

Click Edit > Preferences in the menu and choose Security from the list of icons along the top of the window, so that you see this:

Click the Saved Passwords button and you'll see a list of the websites and corresponding usernames that Firefox has stored in its configuration files. By default the passwords aren't displayed – so that passers-by won't accidentally get a glimpse of your information – but you can enable them with the Show Passwords button.

2 Forget an old password

To force Firefox to forget a password, click it in the list and choose Remove.

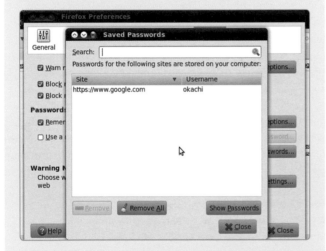

On the subject of security, the Privacy section of the Preferences is also worth exploring. It gives you options to clear your browsing history – that is, web addresses visited, cached files, cookies and login information – from the timeframe of your choice (the last hour, today or all time).

3 Configure cookies

Many websites create 'cookies' when you visit them – small pieces of information so that you can be identified when you return to the site. Some of these, such as your status on an online forum, can be very useful; others, such as those used by advertising companies, can be more invasive. In the Privacy section click 'remove individual cookies' to view them in a list and delete them:

4 Enable Private Browsing mode

Finally, there's a handy way to activate a completely secure, never-to-be-remembered browsing session. In the main Firefox window, click Tools > Start Private Browsing in the menu. An information box will appear to let you know that it's activated. In Private Browsing mode, Firefox doesn't store anything permanently on your computer – no cookies, no cached files, no passwords. When you're done, go to Tools > Stop Private Browsing to return to normal. This is a superb feature if you're using Firefox on someone else's machine, or especially on a public machine in a library, and you don't want traces of your cookies or passwords being left around for prying eyes to discover.

⚠ The wide world of add-ons

Firefox is supported by an ever-growing range of add-ons. These are miniature programs that you can download and run inside the browser that provide extra functionality or change the way the interface works. To find out what's available, click Tools > Add-ons in the main Firefox menu and then click the Browse All Add-ons link in the window that appears. The browser will auto-navigate to the add-ons pages.

There are thousands to explore handling all aspects of the web – social networking, media playback, website construction and much more. You might find a single add-on that massively changes the way you work on the web, so have fun exploring. Here we'll give a mention to some of the add-ons we recommend (they're all free):

Adblock Plus

An extremely powerful tool that effectively eliminates adverts from your browsing experience. This is good if you regularly need to browse websites that drive you insane with adverts, but bear in mind that many sites provide free content due to ads, so they would close down if everyone ran this all the time!

StumbleUpon

This adds a button to your toolbar that you can click to view recommended sites in various categories, such as food, computing and pets. You click the button and you're taken to a random site. But this isn't a ploy to make you spend money – these sites are recommended by other StumbleUpon users in the community, and the more people recommend a site, the more likely it is to come up in the random list. It's a great way to find hilarious and wacky stuff on the web.

FireFTP

If you ever need to transfer files by FTP, this is essential. There are dedicated, standalone FTP clients for Linux, but FireFTP offers virtually every feature you could need: SFTP, SLL encryption, integrity checks, drag-and-drop, file hashing and so forth.

When you've found an add-on that you like, click the green 'Add to Firefox' button and you'll be prompted to install it. If your add-on extends Firefox with major new components you'll find it under the Tools menu.

Advanced Firefox options

Under Edit > Preferences you'll find many other options to tweak: what the home page is, where downloads are stored, how the tab bar behaves, font sizes and so forth. They're all very much self-explanatory so we won't dwell on them here. However, the Preferences screen doesn't include every single setting in Firefox – some are kept back in an advanced mode. In the main Firefox screen, type about:config into the address bar. You'll see a warning that playing around with advanced settings can make the browser unstable, so heed it and click the button to continue. Then you'll see this:

There's not much in the way of help here; some of the items in the list might make sense to you, but it's a good idea to steer well clear of anything you don't recognise. Double-click on an option to edit it: if it's a true/false option then it will simply toggle from one to the other; if it's an option that requires a number or string of letters, you'll be prompted to enter them. Helpfully, when you change a setting it becomes bold in the list, so you know what you've fiddled with if something breaks.

You can use the Filter bar at the top to search for specific items. By default Firefox strives for maximum compatibility with even the oldest of web servers and sites, but unless you're browsing ancient sites from the late 1990s then there are a few options here you can tweak for a small performance boost:

- network.http.pipelining – Change from false to true.
- network.http.pipelining.maxrequests – Change from 4 to 8.
- network.http.max-connections – Change from 30 to 90.
- network.http.max-connections-per-server – Change from 15 to 30.

This won't radically alter your browsing experience, but it smoothes out connections to servers and cumulatively will make everything a bit snappier.

THE INTERNET
Chatting online

Instant messaging is huge: millions of people use it every day. But there's a problem, in that there's no single, standard way of talking to people immediately. Some people use Yahoo Messenger, others use MSN, and then there's Google Chat, AIM and many other systems. Linux, however, removes a lot of this complexity by providing a single application that can talk to many different instant messaging (IM) networks. You don't need a separate program for Yahoo, or MSN, or Google – one application handles it all, and it's called Empathy.

1 Starting Empathy

Click Applications > Internet > Empathy IM Client to start it up:

When it starts up for the first time, it won't know anything about you – eg which network you want to use or your username and password. So you'll see the wizard screen:

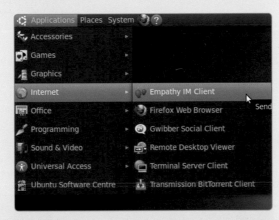

If you've previously been using an instant messaging service and you know your username and password, select the 'Yes, I'll enter my account details now' button and click Forward. If you've never chatted online

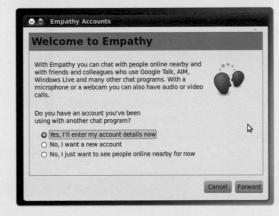

before, you can click 'No, I want a new account' and join the Jabber service. However, Jabber is limited to other Jabber users, so if you'd prefer to be talking to people on, say, the MSN network, then go to www.msn.com in your browser, create an account there and use the details to log in using Empathy. Or for Google, go to http://mail.google.com, create an account and use those details.

2 Enter account details

On the account details screen, you'll see a drop-down box for the type of account you wish to use. It's amazingly comprehensive – Facebook Chat, MySpace, Zephy, ICQ, GaduGadu among many others, along with the more popular services mentioned before. Select the service with which you're signed up and enter your details:

⚠ What about privacy?

At this point you might be concerned about Empathy's privacy. Well, it's all good news: Empathy is a totally open-source, community-supported application. It doesn't connect to any secret services or pass your information around – nothing like that. Empathy's developers have implemented support for all the different messaging systems themselves, so if you're using Google Talk then it connects straight to Google's servers. If you're using MSN then it connects straight to Microsoft's servers. And so forth.

3 Finding friends

Click Forward and Empathy will ask if it can try to find more people for you to talk to:

This is a pretty hit-and-miss affair, and chances are you already know who you want to talk to, so just click Cancel.

4 Viewing your contacts

Then you'll see your Contact List, displaying a list of people who are currently online:

Those users with green speech-bubbles next to their names are currently active in their instant messaging programs – you can speak to them straight away. Those with the gold bubbles containing an arrow are away (they're running the program, but may

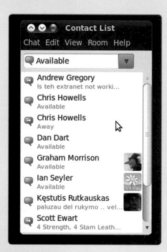

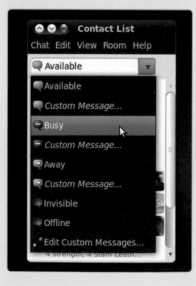

be away from the machine or can't talk right now). Similarly, you can change your status by clicking the drop-down list at the top of the window:

5 Get chatting

To start a conversation, double-click on a name in the contact list and a new dialog box will appear. Click into the bottom panel of the dialog and type what you want to say, and then hit Enter:

If you're viewing a different application when your co-chatter responds, you'll hear a 'bing' sound and a small notification box will appear to make you aware that there's activity in Empathy.

6 Sending files

The program isn't just limited to text-based chatting, though. If the IM service you're using supports it, you can send someone a file by right-clicking on their name in the contact list and choosing 'Send file':

Choose the file you want to send, and a File Transfers dialog box will appear, showing the progress. (The recipient has to agree to receive the file first – you can't just dump random files on to their hard drive!)

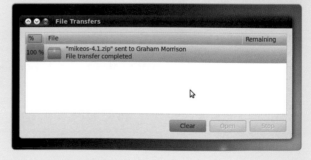

7 Buddy options

There are other options available via right-clicking on a name in the list – you can view previous conversations with them, or remove them from the list entirely. To add a new contact to the list, click into the Chat menu and choose Add Contact. You'll be prompted to enter the account name of the new contact, along with an alias. This alias can be anything you like, and is only stored on your own machine – it's simply a way to give a more personal name like 'Dad' to an identifier like 'davelsmith01'.

8 Multiple accounts

As mentioned earlier, one of Empathy's major strengths is its ability to handle multiple chat networks (aka protocols). What's even better, is that you can have multiple accounts logged in at the same time, and Empathy handles them all seamlessly. Click Edit > Accounts and you can add a new account to go alongside your current one:

Click Add and choose the type of account you want, then enter the login details. When you're done, you'll be logged in twice, and Empathy will cunningly mix together contacts from all of your accounts into the main list. No longer does it matter which network anyone is on – it's all the same to you! (If you need to find out the network that a contact is using, right-click their name and choose Information. The Account line in the resulting dialog box has an icon indicating the network.)

⚠ Too many notifications?

As you spend time with Empathy, you'll probably want to customise its notification system – it might be driving you mad with information, or perhaps it's not telling you enough. Click Edit > Preferences in the menu and then choose the Notifications tab in the dialog box that appears:

Here you can totally disable bubble notifications (the boxes that appear in the corner of the screen when events happen), or request that they're only displayed at certain times, eg when contacts come online. Similarly, under the Sounds tab you can configure Empathy to make noises when all sorts of events happen – messages being received, account connections and so forth. Play around and you'll find a happy level of notifications for you that's not too annoying but keeps you informed of goings-on in the chat world.

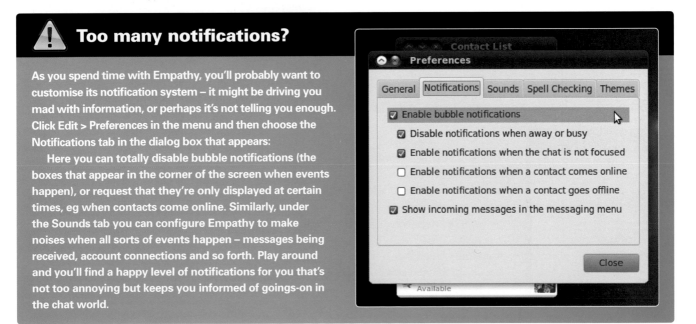

Installing Skype

So, Empathy does a superb job for text-based chat, but what about the most commonly used VoIP (voice over IP) system in the world, Skype? Fortunately, that's supported on Linux.

1 Get the package

Go to www.skype.com in Firefox and navigate to the Download section. There you'll see a list of software packages for various versions of Linux – choose the one for Ubuntu, 32-bit.

When you click the link you'll be prompted to save it, so click Save File.

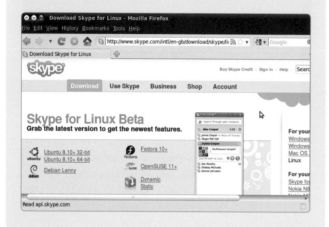

2 Install it

When the download has completed, close Firefox and click Places > Downloads from the desktop menu.

Double-click the Skype package (the file starting with 'skype' and ending in '.deb') to install it:

Click Install Package and enter your password if requested. When it's finished, click Applications > Internet > Skype from the main desktop menu to launch it. You'll be prompted to read the licence agreement, and if you agree you'll see the main login screen:

3 Logging in

If you're already signed up to Skype then just type in your username and password and click Sign in. If not, click the blue link that says 'Don't have a Skype Name yet?' and a dialog box will appear asking for your details.

Once you're logged in, you'll see the main Skype window:

The list of contacts.

4 Checking audio

Plug in your headset and click the green phone icon in the Skype Test Call box to make sure that everything's working. You should hear some audio and then be prompted to record a message to test your microphone. If it all works correctly, you can close the call. If not, click the volume icon in the system tray at the top-right of the desktop and choose Sound Preferences:

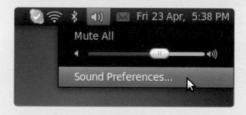

Accessing the sound settings.

In the window that appears, you'll see a slider at the top for the main volume, along with more settings in the tabs. In the Input tab you can monitor the input level – try talking into your microphone and playing with the volume slider to make sure that it's at a decent level. Above all, make sure that everything is unmuted and set to a reasonable level, and then go back to the Skype Test Call to confirm that your new settings work.

There are many other features in Skype beyond the basic calling functionality; click the S button in the bottom-left of the main Skype window to bring up the menu. There you can access options, change your status and sign out.

THE INTERNET
Setting up email

Email predates the worldwide web by many years, but nowadays many people access their inboxes through a web-based front end, such as those provided by Google Mail and Hotmail. There are some upsides to this: you can access your email from any computer, and your messages are all stored remotely on a different server, so if your computer explodes you won't lose any messages.

However, many users prefer to run a dedicated email program on their own machines, rather than using the web. There are some very good reasons for this. Firstly, with a standalone program your messages are stored on your hard drive rather than some random server on the Internet, so you don't need to be connected to the net to read and compose mail. Secondly, with an email program storing your mails locally, you know that you have a private copy of your data. A web-based email operation could close down at any moment (or suddenly start charging money for access), so it's reassuring to know that you can't lose your important data.

The email client included with Ubuntu, called Evolution, is an advanced program that also sports calendaring functionality and other features.

2 Enter your details
Then you'll be asked to enter your name and email address:

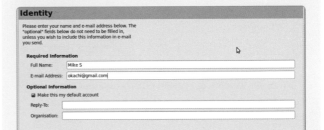

There's also the option to set the 'Reply-To' field in emails that you send. Most people don't need this, but if you want to send out emails from your personal account but have replies sent to your business account, for instance, you can enter the email address of the business account here.

1 Starting Evolution
Launch it via the Applications > Office menu on the desktop. When you run it for the first time, the startup wizard will appear:

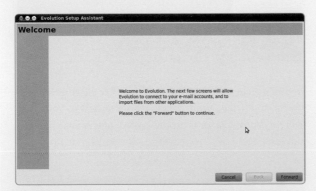

Click Forward to begin. Firstly, Evolution will offer to restore its data from a backup file. Given that you haven't run the program before, you can skip this step, but it's worth remembering that this feature exists for future Linux installations that you may perform. Click Forward to move on to the next screen.

⚠ POP or IMAP

It's important to note that there are two main types of email server on the Internet: POP and IMAP. There are some technical differences in the way that these work, but they're not important to us right now – the most important thing is that we use one of them. Try to find the POP address of your email provider first. As an example, if you're using Yahoo Mail then search the web for 'Yahoo Mail POP access' and in the first few results you'll see information about using POP servers. Reading through we find out that the server is pop.mail.yahoo.com (POP access is only provided for certain accounts).

If you can't find any information about POP, try searching for IMAP instead – your mail provider may offer it as an option. Note that while POP and IMAP are by far the most popular types of mail server, Evolution also supports a few others, like Microsoft Exchange.

You will also need the address of an SMTP server for sending mail. This will almost certainly be specified alongside the POP or IMAP address in your mail provider's documentation – if not, a bit of searching will bring it up.

3 Server information

Click Forward and you'll arrive at this screen:

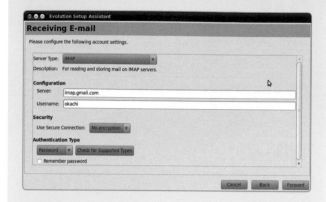

In order to fetch and send email, Evolution needs to connect to your email provider's servers. Depending on the information you entered in the previous screen, Evolution may be able to guess the server name – here, for instance, it knows that the mail server for Google Mail is imap.gmail.com. If it's blank, you'll need to find out the address of the server that your email provider uses.

Choose the type of server you want to use from the drop-down list, and then, after entering in the details, click Forward:

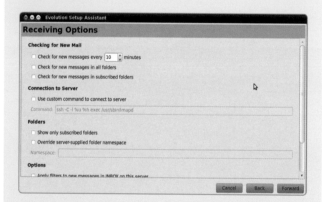

Here you can tell Evolution how often you want it to connect to the mail server and retrieve new messages. If you're using POP you'll see a checkbox that says 'leave messages on server'. If you check this box, you can be guaranteed that you'll always have an online backup of your emails, along with the ones stored on your computer. However, if your online mailbox has very limited space, you'll probably want to leave this box unchecked, so that there's always space on the server to store new mails. (This doesn't apply for IMAP connections – messages are always stored on the remote server unless you specifically delete them.)

4 The outgoing server

Next up is the SMTP screen, where you define the server for outgoing messages:

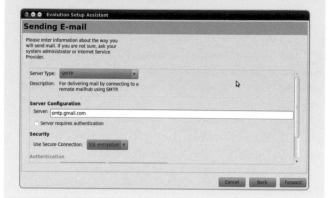

Enter the information you found before and click Forward. You'll then be asked to provide a name for this account (eg Home or Work), and then click Apply to activate the new settings.

5 Evolution's main screen

Then the main Evolution window will appear:

In the toolbar beneath the menu, click the Send/Receive button to retrieve your emails from the server. You will be prompted for your password, and mails will be downloaded from the server to your local machine:

Offline mail management

Earlier on we mentioned one of the advantages that standalone email clients have over their web-based counterparts: offline mail management. You can see this in action by clicking File > Work Offline in the menu. Try composing a new message, clicking Send when you're done. In offline mode, the message won't be sent immediately; instead, it will be stored in a local mailbox, ready to be sent the next time you're connected to the Internet. If you expand the On This Computer mailboxes under the Inbox pane on the left you'll see that there's a new mail in the Outbox. This is the mail that you composed before, waiting in a postponed state.

Click File > Work Online and then the Send/Receive button, and you'll see that email disappear out of the Outbox as it is sent.

One of the biggest headaches with email, especially if your address is publicly viewable (eg on a company website), is spam. Despite all the efforts of Internet service providers around the world, spam remains a major problem for many people, with no signs of slowing down. Fortunately, though, Evolution uses an extremely effective spam-blocking system called Bogofilter that should keep most junk mail at bay.

Bogofilter doesn't just scan your incoming mails for obvious spam-type words and phrases; it actively learns from the mails that you mark or un-mark as spam. For instance, if you click on a message in the Inbox and then go to Message > Mark as > Junk in the menu, it will not only be removed from the Inbox and placed into the Junk folder, but Bogofilter will also learn the words in that email and use them to determine what is and isn't spam in the future.

Don't panic, though: the filter is sensible and errs on the side of caution. Marking a message that contains the word 'happy' as spam won't automatically make all

Once the process has completed you'll see a new expandable section under the Inbox panel on the left, with the name you provided during the set-up stages:

Click on a folder – eg Inbox – to view the messages in the right-hand pane. Voila: your mails are here, ready to read. Click on a message to view it in the panel at the bottom of the window:

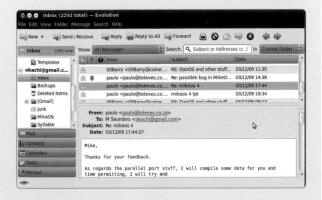

6 Sending a new mail

Performing everyday tasks in Evolution is just like in any other email client, and you won't be perplexed by the interface. Click the New button in the top-left of the screen to compose a new message:

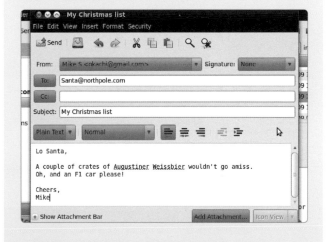

There's nothing surprising here – just type in the address and a subject line, and then what you want to say. The most important widget to note in the window is the Plain Text drop-down list. If you click this you can switch to HTML mode, which provides far more opportunities to customise the cosmetic side of the email (eg with pictures and text formatting), but most users prefer simple, resource-friendly plain text. When you're done, click Send.

other messages containing 'happy' land up in the Junk folder. Rather, the filter will start to recognise patterns and reoccurring words in the mails you've marked as spam.

It also works the other way round: if you look inside your Junk folder after a Send/Receive operation and you find a legitimate piece of mail in there, click it and go to Message > Mark as > Not Junk; Bogofilter will learn that mails like this are not spam and it should be more careful in labelling them as such in the future.

In this way, Evolution's spam filtering system improves the more you use it; and even better, it adapts to your specific Inbox. If you run a small trading business, for instance, you might receive a lot of email that many 'solutions' would instantly brand as spam, but with Bogofilter's ever-growing brain you can fine-tune it to the needs of your Inbox.

Exploring the settings

Back in the toolbar you'll see various other buttons for common operations: replying to a mail, replying to all recipients and forwarding a mail on to someone else. Evolution is a highly configurable mail client – click Edit > Preferences in the menu and use the icons on the left to navigate through the categories of settings:

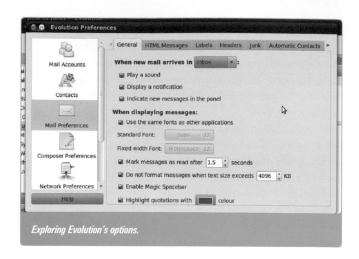

Exploring Evolution's options.

Under Mail Accounts you can customise the login information and server details that you provided earlier, and you can even add more accounts to access multiple mailboxes from the same screen. Meanwhile, under Mail Preferences you can configure how Evolution behaves when new mail is received, such as playing a sound or displaying a message. If you're stumped as to the purpose of a particular option, click the Help button in the bottom-left of the Preferences window.

⚠ The calendaring component

Finally, let's take a quick look at the calendaring facilities. In the main Evolution window you'll find a bunch of buttons in the bottom left for switching between views – Mail, Contacts, Memos and so forth. Click the Calendars button and you'll see a screen similar to this:

At the top-right of the screen you'll see buttons for switching between different views – single day, week or month. To add an event or appointment, right-click on a day and choose New Appointment from the pop-up menu.

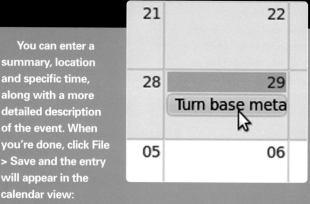

You can enter a summary, location and specific time, along with a more detailed description of the event. When you're done, click File > Save and the entry will appear in the calendar view:

Double-click on an entry to edit it, or right-click and choose Delete to remove it permanently.

This is all good and well for tracking your personal appointments, but you can take it further with Internet integration too. Click Edit > Preferences from the menu and, in the window that appears, select Calendar and Tasks from the list of categories down the left. Then choose the Calendar Publishing tab and click Add.

Most calendaring services use the iCal format for handling data, which Evolution supports. In the Publishing Location tab you can enter the server location and authentication information required to access remote calendars – look in your server's documentation for these details (or, for business accounts, ask your nearest administrator).

THE INTERNET
Using BitTorrent

BitTorrent is one of the most popular ways to share large files over the Internet, without depending on a central resource. It's a peer-to-peer (P2P) system in which bunches of people around the globe share files, so you download a file in chunks from various sources rather than just a single server. You can find out more about how BitTorrent works (and how to set up your own BitTorrent server) in Section 7 – here we'll focus on downloading files.

1 Locating a .torrent file

To start with, you need a .torrent file: a small file that provides information about the full file that you want to download. For instance, say you want to grab a new Linux distribution via BitTorrent. www.linuxtracker.org is a good website for this:

You'll see a list of the most recent Linux distribution releases, or you can search for a specific one that you want to try. (There's a list of the most notable Linux distros in the Appendix of this book.)

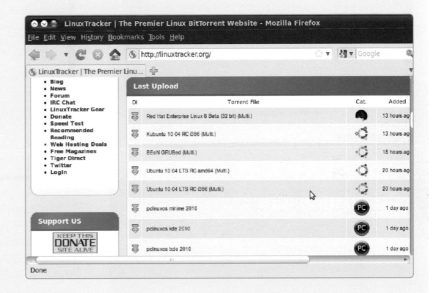

2 Downloading the .torrent

For this example, we're going to grab PCLinuxOS KDE 2010, so we click the link:

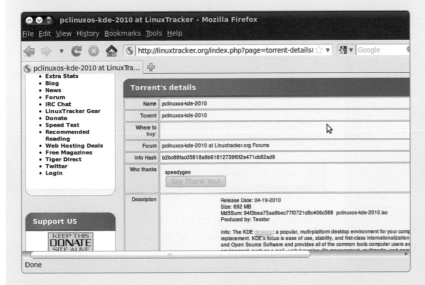

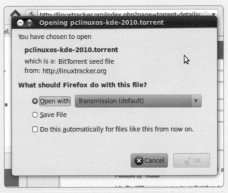

There's various information about what the distro does and its features. Towards the top there's a 'Torrent' link, and when we click it Firefox offers to either save the pclinuxos-kde-2010.torrent file to the desktop, or open it in Transmission, which is the BitTorrent program that's included with Ubuntu.

3 Starting Transmission

Whatever route you take, providing you end up with a .torrent file you can double-click it and Transmission will open, prompting you for confirmation that you want to download the complete file. (Alternatively you can find it under the Applications > Internet desktop menu.)

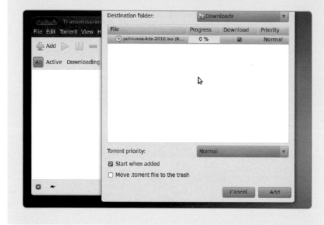

4 Watching the progress

When you click Add, you'll be taken to the main Transmission window as the full file starts being downloaded. You can see a progress bar indicating how much of the download is completed, and a rough estimate of how much time is remaining (based on the current download speed):

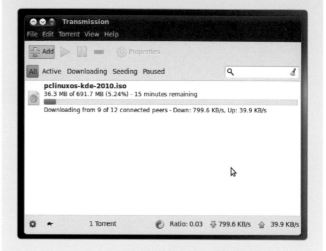

The information line below the progress bar is extremely important here. It tells you how many 'peers' you are downloading the file from – that is, how many other BitTorrent users are providing you with chunks of the file. BitTorrent works entirely on popularity: if a really well-known and well-liked Linux distribution is released, lots of people will be sharing it and therefore Transmission will find more computers to connect to and download chunks of the file from. Conversely, for lesser-known, relatively obscure distros, there may only be two or three people sharing the file, and therefore you'll have fewer sources and slower downloads.

Transmission

Transmission lets you download multiple files at once using different .torrents, and each will have its own status line in the main pane, showing you the number of peers and the download and upload rate for each file. For total download and upload rates, see the bottom panel:

Note the down and up arrows. The down arrow shows the total download rate for all of your torrents, while the up arrow is the total upload rate (for the chunks of the files that you're sharing with other users). Now, sometimes this can expand to saturate your entire connection, especially if

⚠ Sharing files

How exactly do you share a file? You don't – well, not explicitly. Just by downloading something from BitTorrent, you automatically share the chunks that you've downloaded with other users. Simply by being part of the 'swarm' of users grabbing a particular file, you're contributing to the pool of available resources. It's a fantastic system – democratic sharing of data.

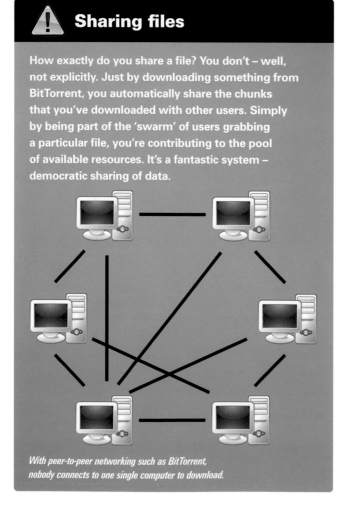

With peer-to-peer networking such as BitTorrent, nobody connects to one single computer to download.

you're downloading multiple torrents and sharing a lot of data with other users. This could make your other Internet apps – eg Firefox – horribly slow. Fortunately there's an easy fix.

Click the cog icon in the bottom-left of the main Transmission window and you'll see this menu:

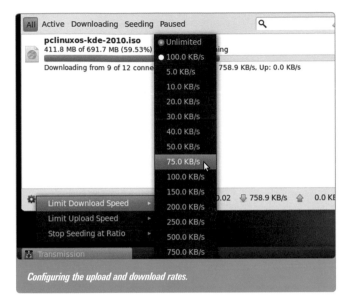

Configuring the upload and download rates.

Here you can choose exactly how much data, in kilobytes per second, that you want to allow for downloads and uploads. The rates you'll want to choose depend on the speed of your connection and how desperate you are to complete your downloads, but by trying various speeds you'll find a happy balance between decent download rates and stutter-free web surfing.

During a download, you can click on a torrent in the main list and use the toolbar buttons to pause it or remove it (use the minus button). When the download is completed, you'll find the full file in the same directory as your .torrent file, and the status line will change:

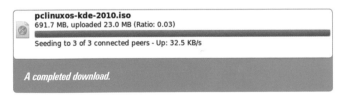

A completed download.

Here you'll see how many peers you're 'seeding' to – that is, how many other computers on the Internet are connected to yours and downloading chunks of the file. It's very good netiquette to leave a file seeding for a while after you've downloaded it, so that others can grab it too. You don't need to do this forever, but if you've spent a couple of hours downloading a large file, it's a good idea to leave it seeding for another couple of hours to help with the file sharing effort. If everyone closed their BitTorrent clients straight after grabbing a file, very soon there would be barely any 'seeders' left!

Exploring Transmission's options

Transmission is a highly configurable program; click Edit > Preferences in the menu to see all of the available options:

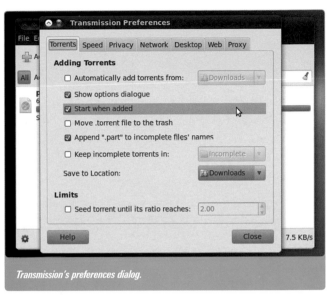

Transmission's preferences dialog.

Use the tabs along the top to navigate through different categories of settings – you can modify network ports, enable encryption and go through a proxy server if necessary. If you're unsure about any particular setting, just leave it as it is; the defaults are perfectly fine for most users.

So that's BitTorrent: you're now empowered to download and share files without being reliant on single servers. There's a vast range of places to get .torrents on the net – just Google what you're looking for (eg 'classical music torrents'). Bear in mind that many files shared by BitTorrent users are copyrighted, though, and this is becoming a big issue with media companies and governments around the world!

BitTorrent sites such as The Pirate Bay have become notorious for sharing copyrighted software.

Office work
04.

In this section

OFFICE WORK
Word processing: Writer

Writer is the word processing component of OpenOffice.org and can be used for everything, from jotting down notes to writing complete books. As with most word processors, it hides a lot of its functionality behind menus and options, so we'll look at the basics first and then explore further. To start Writer, click Applications > Office > OpenOffice.org Word Processor. After a few moments you'll see the main window:

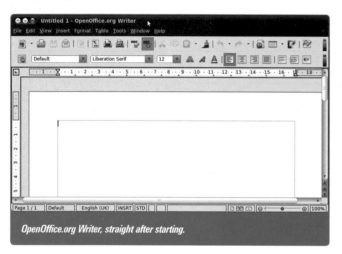

OpenOffice.org Writer, straight after starting.

If you're familiar with Microsoft Office, especially the versions before the introduction of the 'Ribbon' interface, you'll feel straight at home here – the layout is extremely similar. Beneath the menu there's a toolbar providing one-click access to the most-used features in the program, such as opening/saving files, running the spelling checker, undo/redo and so forth. You can find out what any toolbar button does by hovering the mouse pointer over it and reading the tooltip.

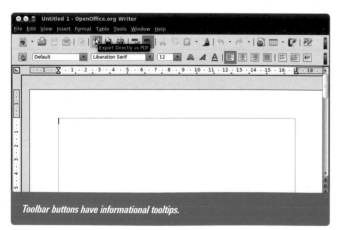

Toolbar buttons have informational tooltips.

Beneath the toolbar you'll see the formatting bar, which lets you change the text style, font family and font size. Beneath that is the ruler and then the document view. Along the bottom you'll find a status panel providing information on the document (page number, language, insert/overwrite mode) along with a slider control that you can click and drag to zoom in and out of the document.

To load a file, click File > Open and navigate to the document you need. When you're finished and want to save your work, click File > Save and a dialog box will pop up. OpenOffice.org can save files in a huge range of formats, which we'll cover later, but for now you can click the 'File type' button and choose the one you want.

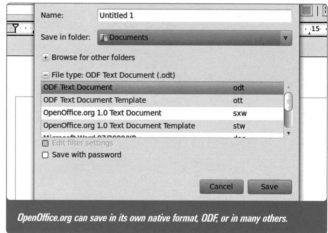

OpenOffice.org can save in its own native format, ODF, or in many others.

As a short cut, you can use the Ctrl+s keys (press at the same time) to save your work. You'll find a full table of keyboard short cuts at the end of this section.

Editing and formatting text

To enter text, just click into the document pane and start typing away. By clicking and dragging the mouse across a portion of text you can highlight it, creating a text selection.

1 Copying and cutting text

Click Edit > Copy to save that portion of text to the clipboard storage area, or Edit > Cut to delete it from the document (but still store it in the clipboard). You can insert text back into the document from the clipboard with Edit > Paste.

2 Using the spelling checker

If you misspell a word or use a word that's not in Writer's dictionary, a red squiggle appears underneath it. You can then right-click on the word and a list of alternatives will appear – but if the word is correct and you want Writer to stop bothering you about it, click Ignore. Alternatively, you can save the word into Writer's dictionary via Add > standard.dic, so it will always remember the word for future sessions.

You can disable this as-you-go spelling checking by turning off the red-underlined 'ABC' icon in the toolbar, and use the normal 'ABC' icon to the left of it to perform a full spelling check when you want.

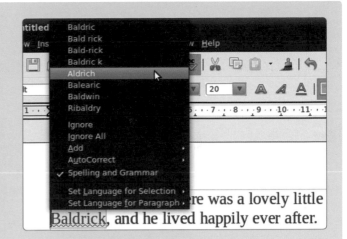

3 Adding formatting to text

Formatting text is very simple. Click and drag with the left button to select the text that you want to change, and then use the features in the second toolbar to change it.

To the right of that you have a drop-down list for the font size, and then buttons to toggle bold, italic and underlined text. After those there are four buttons to change the alignment of the text: left, right, centred and justified.

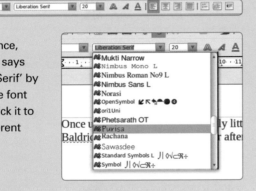

For instance, the box that says 'Liberation Serif' by default is the font selector – click it to choose different font styles.

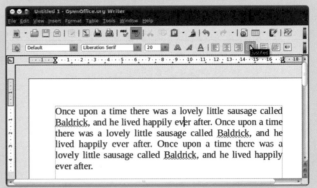

4 Bullet points

After the text alignment buttons, there are buttons for numbered and non-numbered (bullet-point) lists. Click one of these and start typing; you'll see that every time you hit Enter to start a new paragraph, Writer inserts a new number or bullet point. When you're finished with your list, hit Enter twice and the cursor will go back to the edge of the document – as it was originally.

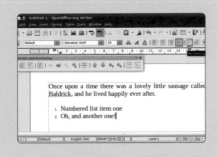

5 Undoing and redoing actions

Two extremely useful buttons in the top toolbar are undo/redo, denoted by orange arrows. Click these to step back and forth through the changes you make in the document – for instance, if you accidentally delete a large chunk of text, click the left-pointing arrow to undo your changes. Next to these buttons you'll find small, black arrows: click them to bring up a list of changes that you can navigate through.

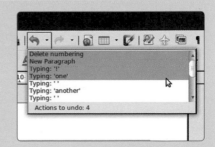

⚠ Headers and footers

Many documents require headers and/or footers – that is, static sections above and below the page content that appear on every page. For instance, you might use the header to print the title on every page, or the footer for a website URL or page number. To enable these features, click the Header tab and check the 'Header on' box:

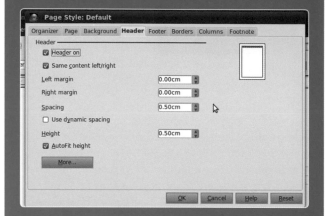

Do the same in the Footer tab if you want the same at the bottom of the page. Now, when you close the Page dialog and go back to your document, you'll see new editable sections at the top and/or bottom of each page. You can click into these boxes and type text, just like anywhere else in the document:

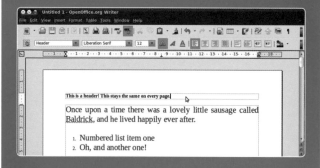

It's important to note that this text is static; it's the same on every page. You can edit it wherever you are in your document, but any changes you make will be updated on all the other pages too.

However, there are a couple of special pieces of text you can add that Writer changes automatically to fit each page. In the header, if you click Insert > Fields > Page Number a grey box with a number will appear. As you scroll through the document, you'll see that it changes with every page. You could also add 'of' and then click Insert > Fields > Page Count so that, for example, '1 of 24', '2 of 24' etc appears on each page of the document.

Document information and settings

To get information on the number of words and characters in your document, click Tools > Word Count. This not only shows information for the entire document, but also the current selection, which is useful if you're working on a large file and need to keep track of the sizes of sections.

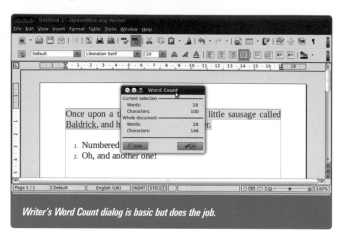

Writer's Word Count dialog is basic but does the job.

By default Writer uses A4 page sizes. You can change this by going to Format > Page and clicking the Page tab in the window that appears:

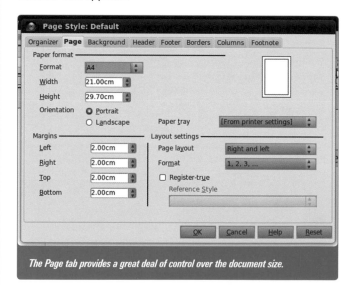

The Page tab provides a great deal of control over the document size.

Use the Format drop-down menu to switch to a different page size, or type in the exact sizes in the Width and Height boxes if you prefer. To switch from portrait to landscape mode (ie rotate the paper by 90°) use the toggle buttons underneath.

With A4 paper, Writer automatically uses margins of 2cm for all the edges of the document. If you're going to print the document on a printer that will happily work right up to the edges of the page, or you're going to generate a PDF (in which case margins don't matter), you can reduce them using the options in the bottom-left of this window.

The power of styles

As you format text in your document, you may want to save a bunch of formatting options for later use. For instance, you might have a particular set of formatting options for captions: 12 point font, bold, and indented by 1cm. If you had to remember these options and apply them every single time you inserted a caption into your document, it would soon become extremely annoying – but thankfully, 'styles' are here to save time.

These are collections of formatting options, and Writer is supplied with a handful.

1 Finding a style

Try selecting some text in your document, and then clicking the left-most drop-down list in the formatting toolbar:

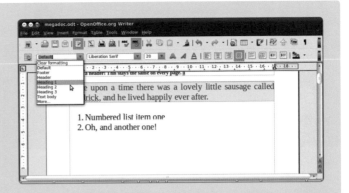

Try them out – you'll see that heading styles tend to be large and bold, whereas the 'text body' style is more plain, as you'd expect normal text to be.

2 Editing a style

You can edit styles by going to Format > Styles and Formatting, or hitting the F11 key. A floating dialog box will appear containing a list of styles available to the document: right-click on a style and choose Modify to change it, or New to create a new one.

A Paragraph Style dialog will appear with a vast array of options, controlling all aspects of text appearance.

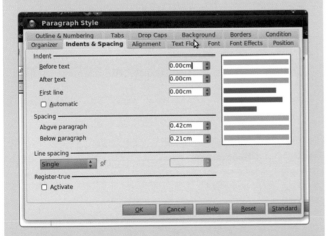

Click around the tabs at the top: you can change the font, indentation, alignment, spacing, borders, colours and more – it's hugely versatile. Give your style a name in the Organizer tab and click OK when you're happy with it. You can now double-click your new style in the list to activate it in the text, and make it prominent in the drop-down list on the toolbar.

3 Creating templates with styles

In the future you might want to create other documents with your new styles, and this is where the templates system comes in. Click File > Templates > Save, provide a name, and the current document (all text and styles) will be saved for future use. To make a new document based on the template, click File > New > Templates and Documents and then choose your template from Templates > My Templates.

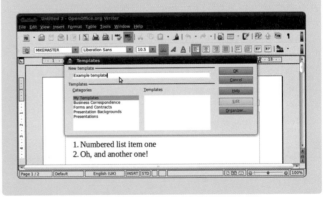

Writer's auto-correction features

As you type text into your document, you'll notice that Writer often tries to correct mistakes or improve your text – for instance, if you type 'teh' then Writer will correct it to 'the'. If you type '(c)' then Writer will insert the copyright symbol. For certain documents these automatic changes can be annoying, so go to Format > AutoCorrect > AutoCorrect Options to see the settings.

In the first tab you'll find the list of automatic replacements for special characters and mistyped words;

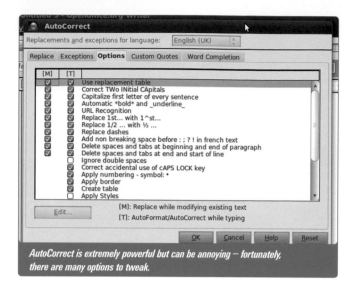

AutoCorrect is extremely powerful but can be annoying — fortunately, there are many options to tweak.

under Options you can change the way Writer attempts to automatically format certain pieces of text. If you want to turn off all AutoCorrect features in one go, just uncheck Format > AutoCorrect > While Typing in the main Writer menu.

Images, tables and printing

Writer isn't just limited to formatted text: you can also use it as a desktop publishing tool with the ability to insert pictures and tables. Let's start with the former.

1 Adding an image

To insert an image into the current document, click Insert > Picture > From File and then choose the picture from your hard drive. If the picture is large, Writer may make it fill up the whole width of the document – if you don't want that, click and drag the green boxes at the corners of the image to resize it. (If you want to keep the proportions the same, hold shift while clicking to resize.) You can then click and drag the smaller image around to place it in the document.

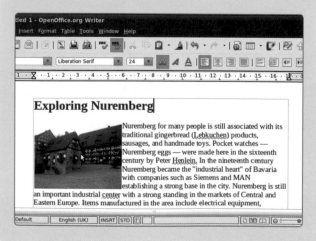

2 Fine-tuning the position

As you can see, the settings here are not ideal: there is no border around the image and therefore the text is extremely close to it. We can fix this by right-clicking on the image and choosing the Picture entry in the pop-up menu. In the dialog box that appears, you can alter the size of the image, fine-tune its position and change the wrap (how text flows around it). To create space around the image, click the Wrap tab and enter the numbers you want for spacing to the left, right, top and bottom.

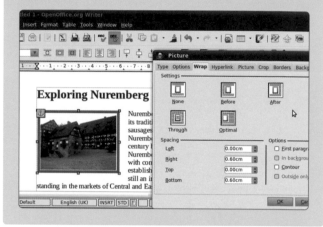

3 Adding a table

To create a table, click Insert > Table and a dialog box will appear, letting you give it a name and choose the number of columns and rows. When you click OK, the table will be inserted at the location of the cursor.

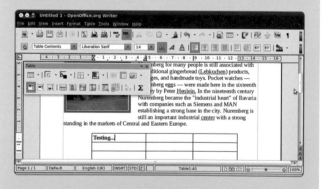

You can click into the cells of the table to type in text, or click on the edges to resize them. To add or remove rows or columns, click into the table and then use the Table menu at the top. For especially advanced documents you can even insert tables inside other tables and change the border style and background colour – right-click in the table and choose 'Table...' from the pop-up menu for further options.

4 Getting a page preview

If you want to make a hard-copy version of your document, you can get an idea of how it will look on the printed page by clicking File > Page Preview.

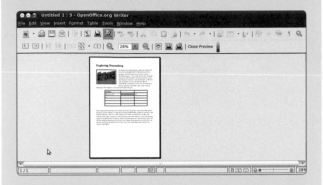

Press Esc or click Close Preview to go back to the document. To print, click File > Print – then choose your printer from the Name list, and if you need to change printer options, click Properties. You can choose the range of pages you wish to print, along with the number of copies. (If Writer doesn't show your printer, click System > Administration > Printing from the Ubuntu main menu at the top of the screen, then click the Add button and choose your printer.)

Exporting files, options and help

By default OpenOffice.org uses the OpenDocument Format, a completely open and free format that any developer can use in their software. (Contrast this with Microsoft Office formats, which tend to include big chunks of binary data that are a mystery to anyone outside of Redmond.) For normal day-to-day work, we recommend using OpenDocument Format (.odt in Writer) to store your files, as you can be guaranteed that it'll be well supported for many years to come.

However, if you need to share files with users or offices that are running Microsoft's suite, you will need to use a format that they can read. When saving a file, click the 'File type' button and scroll down past the OpenOffice.org options. You'll see that there are various versions of Microsoft Word available – if you save in the first, 97/2000/XP, your file will be readable on all recent versions of the suite.

Further down in the file type options you will see Microsoft Word 2003 and 2007 XML. These document formats are not as well supported as 97/2000/XP – ie some formatting options and layout features in your document may be lost – so we don't recommend using them as yet.

Outside of word processors, Writer lets you export to two more formats: HTML and PDF. The first is useful if you want to make a web page version of your document, and the latter generates a file that can't be edited, but will look exactly as it

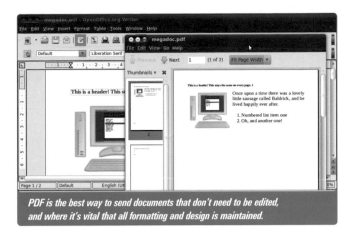

PDF is the best way to send documents that don't need to be edited, and where it's vital that all formatting and design is maintained.

does on your screen on any other computer that has a PDF reader. We recommend using PDF for such documents as invites and CVs, where you don't want a random version of Microsoft Office playing games with the formatting!

Click File > Export and then choose whether you want HTML or PDF. For the latter you'll see various options relating to image compression and security – if you're familiar with the workings of PDF documents you can alter these, but otherwise the defaults are fine. Once you've generated the PDF file, double-click it in the file manager to look at it; the results should be identical to the document you edited.

Finally, some pointers to extra options and information: you can find Writer's gargantuan settings dialog in Tools > Options. Down the left-hand side you'll see boxes with plus signs, which you can click to open up even more settings. For instance, if you want to change the default document language to something other than English (or a different variant of English), expand the Language Settings option and click Languages.

Most features of Writer are modifiable through the suite's normal menus, but if you want to delve further then the vast wealth of options here will keep you busy for a few days. To access the help facilities built into Writer, click Help > OpenOffice.org Help. You can then search for anything you need assistance with – eg images, margins, printing etc.

⚠ ESSENTIAL SHORT CUTS

Save file	Ctrl+s	Italic text	Ctrl+i
Print	Ctrl+p	Align left	Ctrl+l
Exit	Ctrl+q	Align centre	Ctrl+e
Undo	Ctrl+z	Align right	Ctrl+r
Redo	Ctrl+y	Justify	Ctrl+j
Find/replace	Ctrl+f	Page break	Ctrl+Enter
Bold text	Ctrl+b	Styles	F11
Underline text	Ctrl+u	Get help	F1

OFFICE WORK
Spreadsheets: Calc

Whereas word processors are designed to deal with text, spreadsheets are created specifically for handling numbers. If you've never used a spreadsheet before you may wonder why we're covering it here – after all, only big businesses with huge stacks of data need to use spreadsheets, right? Not so: you can use a spreadsheet for all manner of day-to-day tasks, such as managing your home finances or keeping track of items in a collection.

OpenOffice.org's spreadsheet program, Calc, is visually very similar to Microsoft Excel and includes many of the same features. If you're proficient in Excel then you won't have any trouble navigating around the program.

1 Starting Calc
Click Applications > Office > OpenOffice.org Spreadsheet to start it, and when it has loaded you'll see an empty spreadsheet:

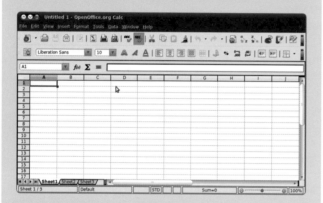

This sheet is arranged as a grid of boxes, or 'cells', in which you can input numbers and data – more on that in a moment. Each cell has a location (aka 'reference') on the sheet: for example, the cell in the top-left is A1, and the one beneath it is A2, and so forth.

2 Exploring the interface
Beneath the menu bar sits a toolbar containing quick access to some of the most common operations: saving files, printing, generating PDFs, undo/redo and others. Beneath that you'll find a formatting toolbar, very similar to the one in Writer – it lets you customise the font style, add bold/italics/underline, and justify the text in a cell.

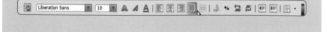

3 Opening files
If you want to open an existing spreadsheet, just click File > Open from the menu and locate it on your drive. Click the 'All files' drop-down box to view the file formats that OpenOffice.org can open: as you scroll down you'll see that it can read spreadsheets from Microsoft Excel 4.0 through to XP, along with the XML format introduced in Excel 2007.

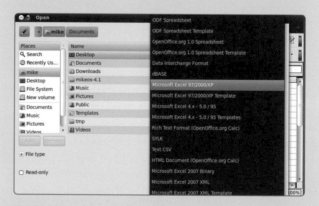

Calc's import facilities are excellent and you should have no problems reading most spreadsheets generated by Excel; nonetheless, because most versions of Excel use a closed binary format for their files you can't be guaranteed that every little bit of formatting or style will work. That's why totally open formats like ODF are so important – they ensure that data is fully readable forever!

⚠ Zooming around

At the bottom-right of the Calc window you'll find a slider that lets you set the zoom level of the document. If you create an especially large spreadsheet, you can zoom out and get a better overview of it.

Entering data and formatting

To enter data into your spreadsheet, just click into a cell and start typing. You can type in text, numbers or a combination of both. When you're finished with a cell, you can hit Enter to move to the cell beneath, or tab to move to the cell to the right. In this way you can enter data without having to keep reaching over for the mouse and clicking into individual cells.

The best way to demonstrate the features of a spreadsheet is with a real-world example, so let's create a sheet for a small home business to calculate income over a yearly period.

1 Set up the sheet

In cell A1 (at the top-left), type 'Month', and in cell B1 (to the right of it) type 'Profits'. In the left-hand column, type the months of the year into the cells beneath, and in the right some random numbers that could be takings for a business. Your end result should look something like this:

2 Add some flair

So far so good, but we could make it look better. For starters, we could make the 'Month' and 'Profit' cells – the headers for each column – stand out more. Click on cell A1 and, still with the mouse button held down, drag the mouse over to B1, so that both are selected, then release the mouse. You'll see that both have been selected as they receive a shaded background:

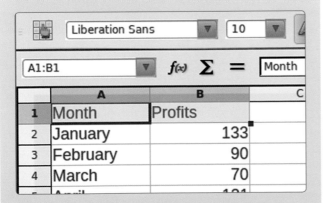

Now use the formatting toolbar to make the cells stand out more. For instance, increase the font size using the drop-down list (the default is 10 point) and make the text bold, italic or underlined using the three 'A' buttons on the toolbar.

3 Resize the columns

There's more we can do, though. Our spreadsheet is only comprised of two columns, so there's a lot of wasted space on the page and the data is looking a bit cramped there. If you hover the mouse on the lines between the column markers at the top of the sheet, you'll see that the cursor turns into a left–right arrow. You can then click and drag to change the width of the columns:

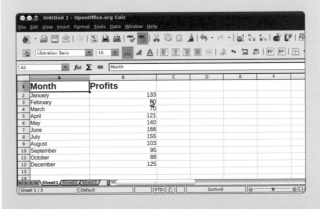

You can do the same in the rows on the left: in the lines between '1' and '2', and '2' and '3', and so forth, click and drag to make rows bigger or smaller. Here's a handy trick: if you want to automatically resize a row or column so that it fits exactly to the largest cell in the row/column, double-click the separator line and it will snap to the appropriate size.

Calculate data with functions

So far we have our data arranged in a grid, but that's nothing particularly special: we could have achieved the same result in Writer using its table facility. Where Calc (and other spreadsheets) comes to life, however, is with the 'function' features. Essentially, a function is a special code that represents a calculation in the document. For instance, click into an empty cell and type:

=9*50

You'll see that the cell now contains 450, the result of nine times fifty. By putting the equals (=) sign before a number or calculation, we tell Calc to use the result of the calculation in the cell, and not just print what we've typed in. When you select the cell with the mouse, you'll see the function definition in the bar just above the sheet – you can click in there to edit it:

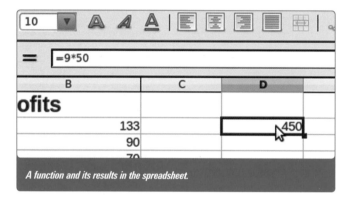

A function and its results in the spreadsheet.

Now, functions can refer to other cells as well as raw numbers. If you change the function to =B2*2, for instance, it will show the value of cell B2's contents multiplied by two:

*Cell B2 contains 133 here, so the function =B2*2 produces 266.*

The power of functions stems from the fact that they're constantly updated. If you change the number contained within cell B2, all functions that reference it – like the one we've just created – will be updated too, and the cell contents changed to reflect it. In this way, spreadsheets go way beyond static documents and become living, working entities, with calculations going on in the background as you update the figures.

Much of the time, you'll want to perform functions on a range of cells, and not just a single one. For instance, in our profit spreadsheet we might want to add a row at the bottom that totals up the profits for the whole year. In cell A13, beneath the list of months, type 'Total', and in cell B13, to the right of it, type:

=SUM(B2:B12)

There are two things at work here: B2:B12, two cells with a colon in between, specifies a range of cells. In this case, we want to use all cells from B2 to B12 (inclusive), which are the cells containing the profit figures in our spreadsheet.

We wrap this up in SUM(), which is a function to sum up – add up – all of the numbers in the range. So =SUM(B2:B12) means 'Add up the contents of cells B2 to B12 inclusive, and show the result'. Because this is a function, the result will be updated immediately when the data for the months changes – try editing, for instance, the value for July and see what happens.

Let's add another row. In A15 type 'Average', and in B14 type:

=AVERAGE(B2:B12)

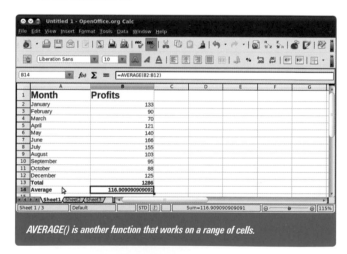

Using a function to generate a total.

AVERAGE() is another function that works on a range of cells.

You'll see that the cell now displays the average of B2 to B12 – in other words, the average monthly profit over the year. There are many more functions included in Calc – hit F1 to open the help window and type 'functions' into the search term box to explore them. In particular, look at the 'mathematical functions' category.

Prettify your data with charts

A picture says a thousand words, and a chart or graph is a great way to express the contents of a spreadsheet in a more attractive, immediately understandable fashion. OpenOffice.org includes a range of different chart types, but first it needs to know which data it is going to work with.

1 Select the data source

Click and drag to select cells A1 to B12 – in other words, all of the cells except for the 'Total' and 'Average' rows, like this:

We're avoiding 'Total' and 'Average' because we just want to make a chart based on the monthly figures, without the large total value messing it up.

2 Access the chart dialog

With the right cells selected, click Insert > Chart from the menu and this dialog box will appear:

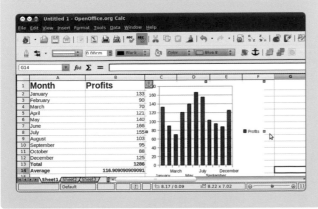

Here you can see all the different types of chart that Calc offers. For now, just click Finish and you'll see the chart inserted into your spreadsheet like this:

3 Reposition the chart

Let's tidy this up a bit. Click and drag the green boxes around the chart to resize it, and click and drag in the centre to position it so that it looks and fits better on the sheet. Try editing the numbers in the profits column – you'll see that the chart is updated immediately.

4 Add another dimension

We can make this chart much prettier: click on it and press delete to get rid of it, and then highlight the data as described before and click Insert > Chart. This time, select Pie from the 'chart type' list, and then select the '3D Look' checkbox. Click Finish and you'll see a much more attractive chart, this time in pie format, showing each month as a segment of a circle.

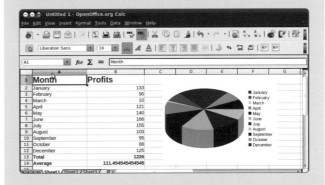

Try exploring the different chart types and options – some are more suited to certain types of data, but they all have their strengths. In a large spreadsheet it's a good idea to vary the charts, in order to give each section its own particular look and feel.

⚠ Saving your work

Click File > Save to save your spreadsheet. The default file format is the aforementioned ODF, which is the best thing to use for your personal documents. If you have to share a spreadsheet with a Microsoft Office user, choose Microsoft Excel 97/2000/XP for maximum compatibility. Of course, not all computers will have the same fonts – and this is especially true when you're sharing files across different operating systems – so the cosmetic side of your spreadsheet may vary slightly when it's viewed on a Windows machine.

As with Writer, you can click File > Export as PDF to generate a PDF document of your spreadsheet.

OFFICE WORK
Presentations: Impress

Presentations typically have two uses: in business, they're a way of taking deathly dull statistics and charts and making them look somewhat interesting so that your audience doesn't fall asleep. (In fairness, you might have something really astonishing to announce to your colleagues, in which case the facts themselves will take priority over the presentation!)

For home users, presentation software is an excellent way to piece together bits of information into one flowing document: for instance, you could make a presentation showing pictures and information from a holiday trip, or from a recent event in your community. OpenOffice.org's presentation tool, Impress, is equipped for both of these types of documents – business and personal – and can be found under Applications > Office > OpenOffice.org Presentation.

In this section we'll step through the process of creating a presentation based on a holiday.

1 Meeting the Wizard
After starting Impress you'll see the Wizard dialog:

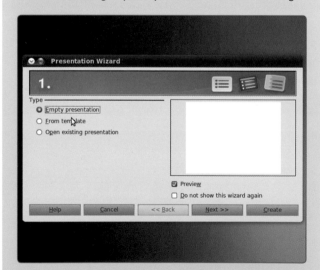

You can create an 'empty' presentation which lets you start from scratch with totally blank slides, but to save time we'll use the templates supplied with Impress – that is, pre-designed presentation frameworks into which we can insert our words and pictures.

2 Choosing a template
Click the 'From template' option and then click some of the templates that appear in the list below. You'll see previews of the templates on the right. We want to use soft colours and have a mention of Ubuntu in the corner of each slide – as a way of promoting Linux! – so click HumanUbuntu in the list and then the Create button. Then the main Impress window will appear:

3 Other template styles
Presentations are composed of slides: individual pictures making up the whole document. At first we only have one slide, and Impress positions it in the centre of the screen, ready for us to modify. On the left-hand panel you can see a thumbnail image of the first slide. On the right-hand panel is a layout selector. You can see that the default slide layout is a title with a bulleted list; try the layout option to the right of it for a two-column design:

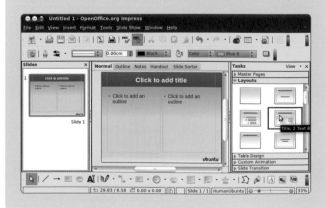

4 Adding your own text

For now, though, let's stick to the original single-column layout. Inside the slide you'll see dotted boxes: these are text boxes, so you can simply click inside them to modify the text that they contain. Click into the title box and type the title of your presentation, then click into the bulleted list box and add a couple of lines of text:

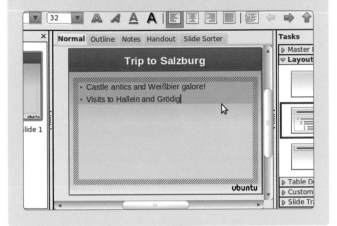

5 Exploring the toolbar

As with Writer and Calc, you can use Undo and Redo under the Edit menu to step back and forth through your modifications. When you're editing text you'll see this toolbar just above the slide:

This is much the same as Writer's toolbar, and lets you format the text that you're editing. From left to right: font family, font size, bold, italic, underline, shadow, left align, centre align, right align, justify and bullet points. (There are other options in the toolbar – hover the mouse over them for tooltips explaining what they do.) You can use these features to spruce up your text.

6 Manipulating text boxes

When you're editing a text box, you'll see that a patterned border appears around it. Click on this border and you'll see turquoise boxes appearing at the edges: these let you resize the text box. If you simply want to move the text box, click and drag on the patterned border area.

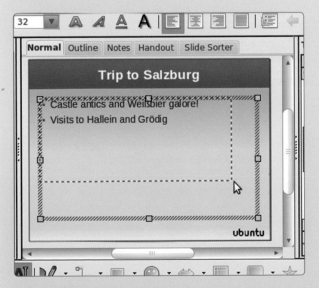

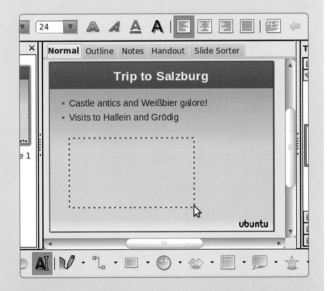

Along the bottom of the window, beneath the slide, you'll see a toolbar that starts with a mouse pointer icon. The icons to the right of this let you add more features to the slide: for instance, you can draw lines, arrows, boxes and circles. Click on the icon and then click and drag on the slide to draw. If you want to add another text box to your slide, click on the icon that says 'A' with a text cursor next to it, and then click and drag on the slide to create the text box to your desired size.

7 Inserting pictures

So, at this stage we can customise the textual content of the slide to our heart's content, but what about images? To add a picture to the slide, click Insert > Picture > From File in the menu and then choose the image you want from the file selector.

Impress will probably just drop the image straight into the middle of your slide, which usually isn't appropriate, so click and drag the green boxes around the edges to resize the image. (Tip: to keep the proportions of the image intact while resizing it, hold shift while clicking and dragging the boxes.) You can move the image by clicking in the middle of it and dragging.

8 View a slide show

Now the first slide of our presentation is intact. You can view it by clicking Slide Show > Slide Show in the menu, or pressing F5. Press Esc to return back to the editor.

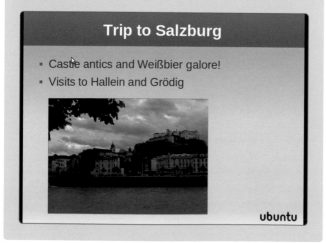

9 Adding more slides

A presentation with a single slide isn't the most exciting thing in the world, so let's add some more. In the left-hand thumbnail panel, right-click in a blank area after the first slide and a pop-up menu will appear, letting you create a new slide.

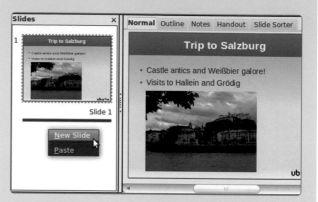

After this you will see a new slide in the main pane, based on the template you chose originally. You probably won't want all slides to look identical, so use the Layouts panel on the right to try some different options. When you're satisfied, go ahead and add your text and images. You can switch back and forth between the different slides in your presentation using the thumbnails in the left-hand pane.

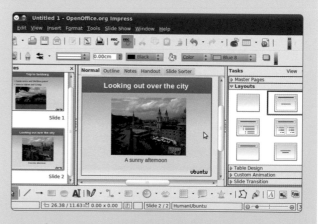

Let's see how this new presentation works as a slide show. Click slide 1 in the left-hand pane and then press F5 to start the presentation. The first slide will appear in full-screen mode, waiting for your input; click anywhere on the screen to advance to the next slide. You can also press the space bar or Enter key to progress through the slides. After the second slide in our two-slide presentation, you'll return back to the editor.

Add spice with transition effects

No matter how pretty the design of a slide is, the presentation looks rather jarring when new slides just appear suddenly on top of the previous one. There's a way we can make this much more favourable to the eyes: using transitions. These are animation effects used to make the switch between slides more smooth and attractive. If you've ever had to sit through a long corporate presentation then you'll know that fancy transition animations can sometimes be overkill, but ultimately it's all a matter of taste!

To set the transition effect that's used when a slide is displayed, click the slide in question in the left-hand panel and then go to Slide Show > Slide Transition in the menu. Now, on the right-hand pane, you'll see a list of different effects, starting with 'No Transition' and then moving on to 'Wipe Up', 'Wipe Right' and so forth. Try scrolling down the list and clicking on the different effects – you will see a preview of them in the main slide view:

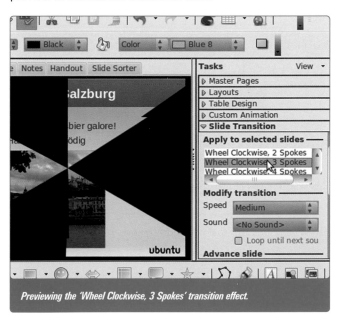

Previewing the 'Wheel Clockwise, 3 Spokes' transition effect.

With your transition selected, hit F5 to view the slide show again, and this time you'll see it in all its full-screen glory. Click on slide two and select a different transition, and then run the slide show again.

Some effects are especially suited to certain types of slides: for instance, if you're going to reveal a particularly amazing piece of information, choose 'Split Vertical Out'. This generates an effect somewhat similar to curtains being opened on a stage. For presentations involving holiday or family photos, you'll probably want something less dramatic and more gentle, so try the 'Fade Smoothly' option. If you're making a business presentation and have to deliver it many, many times, choose the 'Random' option which will save you from being bored silly.

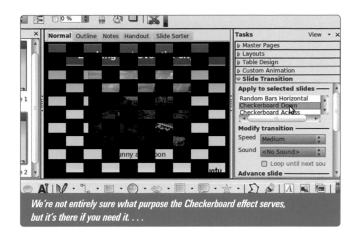

We're not entirely sure what purpose the Checkerboard effect serves, but it's there if you need it. . . .

As well as complete slide transition effects, you can add animation effects to individual elements on a slide too. For example, imagine that you have a slide containing three text boxes, and each of these boxes is of supreme importance.

If you just throw the whole slide on to the screen at once, some people in your audience might start by reading the third box point; others may land their eyes on the second, and so on. Using individual element animation you can make those boxes appear one by one, with each click, thereby making sure that the audience is always focused on one specific fact.

Let's try this out. Go back to slide 1 and click to select the bullet-pointed text box. Then go to Slide Show > Custom Animation in the menu, and look at the pane on the right-hand side. Click Add and a list of animation effects will appear. Scroll around and click them to try them – you'll see the effect previewed in the main view.

Here we're using the 'Boomerang' effect for the initial text box – in this screenshot it's in the middle of its spinning animation.

Note that these are just the animations for making the text appear: via the Exit tab at the top of the Custom Animation window you can also set an effect to be used when leaving the slide. Additionally, while we've only applied the effects to a text box here, you can also apply them to images.

Handling files and exporting your work

So, after following this section you can now create presentations based on templates, edit and format text, insert images, manage slides and create effects for both slide transitions and individual elements. Let's finish off with some information on files and exporting.

As with other components of OpenOffice.org, Impress is capable of reading Microsoft Office documents – in this case, Microsoft PowerPoint. By default Impress saves in ODF format, but you can save the file in .ppt (PowerPoint) format for Windows machines by going to File > Save, then clicking 'File type' and choosing 'Microsoft PowerPoint 97/2000/XP' from the drop-down list.

If you want to put your presentation online, Impress includes a couple of excellent features to help you. Firstly, it can generate an HTML version of your presentation that you can upload to your web host. To see how it will look, click File > Preview in Web Browser. After a few moments, Firefox will appear showing the first slide, with links at the top to navigate between the slides:

The slides are stored as images, and being purely HTML and picture based you won't get the fancy effects and animations that we described earlier. To generate the web version in Impress, click File > Export from the menu, select the folder in which you want to save the files and choose HTML from the file type list. Then click Create in the dialog box that appears. Now go to the folder where you saved the files and open img0.html to start viewing. To put the presentation online, just upload all the files in the folder to your web host.

Another option is SWF, Adobe's Flash format. Click File > Export and choose Macromedia Flash from the file type list to generate a .swf file. Then open that file in Firefox and you'll see the results. Click on the slides to progress through them – again, this doesn't have the neat animation effects, but it does mean that everyone on the planet with a web browser and the Flash plugin will be able to view your presentation. (If you haven't got the Flash plugin installed, see Section 3, The Internet.)

Previewing a web-based version of the presentation.

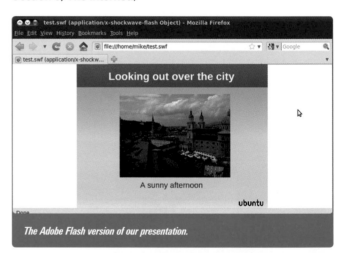

The Adobe Flash version of our presentation.

⚠ Exporting to PDF

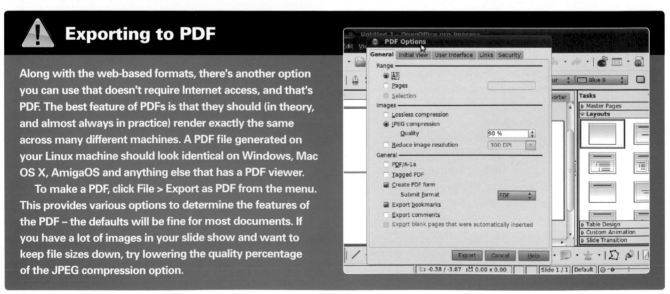

Along with the web-based formats, there's another option you can use that doesn't require Internet access, and that's PDF. The best feature of PDFs is that they should (in theory, and almost always in practice) render exactly the same across many different machines. A PDF file generated on your Linux machine should look identical on Windows, Mac OS X, AmigaOS and anything else that has a PDF viewer.

To make a PDF, click File > Export as PDF from the menu. This provides various options to determine the features of the PDF – the defaults will be fine for most documents. If you have a lot of images in your slide show and want to keep file sizes down, try lowering the quality percentage of the JPEG compression option.

OFFICE WORK
Databases: Base

While Calc is good for juggling numbers, Base comes to life when handling large amounts of data in both textual and numerical format. This database program is designed to efficiently and reliably store data that you can search through and manipulate. If you've never used a database before, you might be thinking that their domain is big-iron, industrial strength servers that rumble along in specialised data-centres. Well, that is true for large installations such as e-commerce websites, but databases also have their place on the desktop.

Currently, the most well-known desktop database software is Microsoft's Access, part of the Office suite. OpenOffice.org's Base program is very similar, in that it provides a graphical front-end to databases so that you don't have to enter cryptic strings of characters at the command line. Here we'll step through the process of creating a database to manage a personal collection (eg DVDs) and then show you how you can take it further.

1 Install Base

To install Base, click Applications > Ubuntu Software Centre and type 'base' into the search box in the top-right of the window. Scroll down and click on the OpenOffice.org Database item in the list and then the Install button inside it; then Base will be downloaded and installed.

3 New database

We want to create a new database, so click the Next button at the bottom. At the following screen you'll be asked if you want to 'register' the database (ie make it active and ready to use), so accept the default option and click Finish.

Lastly, you'll be prompted to name the database – so call it 'My books' or similar. Base will then create a new, empty database and present you with the main screen of the application:

2 Launch the app

Once the installation is complete, close the Software Centre and then launch Base by going to Applications > Office > OpenOffice.org Database in the desktop menu. The Database Wizard will appear:

4 Explore the interface

Down the left-hand side you can see four icons. These represent the different ways of interacting with the database. Tables are the grids used to store the data, and that's what we'll be focusing on in this guide. (Queries is used to search the data, while Forms lets you design attractive front-ends to the database. As the name suggests, Reports generates reports from the contents of the database.)

In Tables, click Create Table in Design View under the Tasks panel and this window will appear:

5 Creating data columns

A table is a bit like a spreadsheet, but we have to be very explicit about the type of data we can store in it. As per our book collection example, in the left-hand 'Field Name' column type ID, Name, Author, Year and Pages (one in each row) so that the result looks like this:

Under the 'Field Type' column we choose the type of data to store. You can see that Base defaults to 'Text [VARCHAR]', which means text of a varying length. That's fine for the Name and Author bits of data, but for the ID, Year and Pages we need to store pure numbers. (Every book in the database will have to have a unique identification number, so that's what the ID field is for.)

Click into the ID, Year and Pages boxes under the Field Type column and a list of data types will appear – choose 'Integer [INTEGER]' for them (which means whole numbers). The result will be like this:

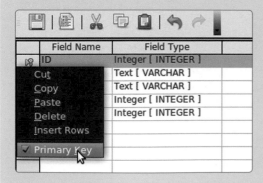

To make sure that no two books can have the same ID, right-click in the small box to the left of ID and check the Primary Key option in the pop-up menu:

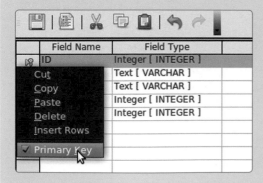

6 Back to the tables view

So, we've created the table that defines the structure of our data – click File > Save and give it a name (eg 'Books') and then close the window. Back in the main Base screen, you'll see that there's now a 'Books' entry under the Tables pane:

Double-click the Books icon and you'll arrive at this screen:

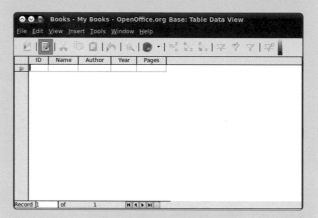

This is waiting for us to add information to the table, so you can start inserting the information for your book collection. As a test, enter three books for now, each with a unique ID. Click the dividers between columns to stretch them out if the interface is too cramped. Eventually you'll have a screen like this:

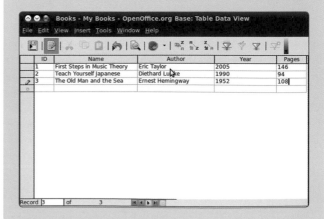

7 Generate a report

When you're done, click File > Save current record and then close the window. Now we're ready to make a report, to see our database contents in a more attractive fashion than the grids. Back in the main Base window, click the Reports button on the left and then the 'Use Wizard to Create Report' icon under the Tasks pane. This window will appear:

Under the 'Available fields' panel you'll see the bits of data that we can show in our report – currently none are in the 'Fields in report' panel, so click Name to select it and then the '>' (single right arrows) button to move it over. Do the same for Author, Year and Pages.

Click Next at the bottom, and you can provide longer alternatives to the short field descriptions we created earlier. For instance, we used 'Year' in the table because it's short, but in the report you might want something more verbose, in which case you can enter 'Year of publication' or similar.

Click Next to move on to the Grouping stage, which we don't need to alter, and then Next again for Sort options. Here you can choose how the contents of the database are sorted in the report – for instance, click the drop-down list that says 'undefined' and choose which one you want (name, author, year etc):

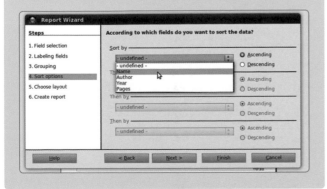

8 View the report

Finally, click Finish and your report will appear in a new window:

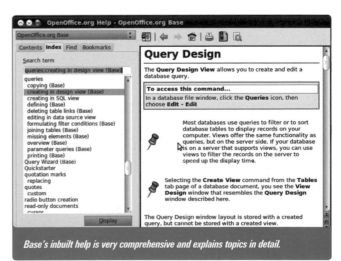

Here we can see the contents of the database in a neatly formatted document, ready for printing or transferring around the Internet (click File > Export to PDF).

Forms and queries

This book collection is a simple example of what can be achieved with a database, but there's a lot more you can do as well, if you're interested in getting more involved with databases. As mentioned earlier, the Forms section lets you create interfaces with buttons, menus and other widgets for manipulating the data, so that you can create a user-friendly front-end to a complex database. The Queries section lets you construct powerful questions that probe the database for certain types of data. For instance, if your book collection contains 300 entries, you could create a query that says 'Show me all of the books that were published between 1970 and 1980 that are more than 200 pages' and display the results accordingly.

For more information on Forms and Queries, hit F1 to bring up the help window and start searching – there's a wealth of information available.

Base's inbuilt help is very comprehensive and explains topics in detail.

05. Multimedia

MULTIMEDIA
Music: Rhythmbox

Audio CDs have managed to stay alive for a lot longer than many people expected, but there's no doubt that we're increasingly moving away from optical media and more towards file formats such as MP3. In a moment we'll show you how to convert your CDs to files stored locally on your hard drive, but for now we'll focus on Rhythmbox, the music player and manager that's included with Ubuntu.

First of all, an important point: Ubuntu doesn't play MP3 files in its default configuration. The reasons for this are complex and rather boring, but in a nutshell the creators of the MP3 format claim various patents on the technology, and many Linux distributors don't want to kick off potentially long-lasting legal battles. Consequently, to stay on the safe side they don't include MP3 support; but end-users can easily enable it.

1 Launch Rhythmbox
To get started, click Applications > Sound & Video > Rhythmbox Music Player from the desktop menu:

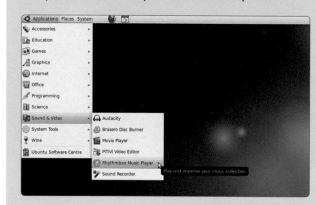

When the main window appears, you'll see that it informs you that it can't play MP3 files:

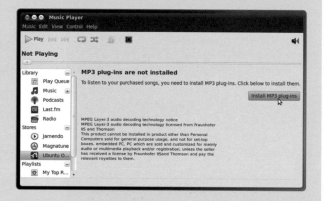

2 Get the plugins
Make sure that you're connected to the Internet and click the Install MP3 plugins button. You may be prompted for your password. Then the necessary files to play MP3 music will be downloaded and installed from the Internet:

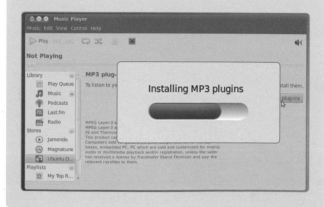

3 Access the library
When the process has finished, click Music under the Library listing in the left-hand panel:

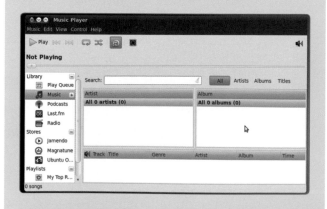

It's all rather empty at present – there's no music in the collection.

4 Add new tunes

To get it started, use the file manager (Places > Home Folder) to navigate to music on your hard drive or an external device. Select the MP3 files that you want and drag them into the bottom panel of the Rhythmbox window:

5 Play your music!

You'll see that the files now appear in the bottom panel along with any information that they store such as artist and album (these are specified by ID3 tags in the file). Double-click an entry in the list to start playing it:

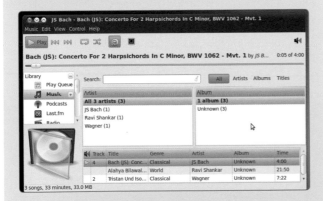

If you can't hear anything, check the volume levels using the speaker icon in the top-right of the Rhythmbox window, and also the master volume control in the system tray (the volume icon next to the envelope and date).

Use the Play button in the toolbar to play and pause music, and the left and right arrow buttons to navigate between tracks. To the right of those buttons you'll see two more buttons for controlling whether songs are repeated or played in a random order – hover the mouse over them for tooltips explaining more.

⚠ Playlists

Over time, as your music collection grows, you'll need better ways to navigate around rather than just scrolling through the list. A quick solution is to use the search box to narrow down your options – type an artist or keyword and only the relevant songs will appear in the list. Another solution – more long-term – is to use playlists. Scroll down to the bottom of the left-hand panel and you'll see that there are three playlists automatically created:

Viewing the existing playlists.

You can put any music tracks you want into a playlist, but they're especially useful for categorising music – for instance, you might have a 'smooth' playlist for relaxing in the evening, or a 'workout' playlist for when you're doing something energetic or demanding and want to be fired up.

To create a new playlist, click Music > Playlist > New Playlist and type in a name. Then select the Music view from the top of the left-hand panel, and click and drag tracks into the playlist:

Then, when you click on the playlist, you'll see only the songs that it contains. You can change the order of songs in the list by clicking and dragging them; to remove a song, right click on it and choose **Remove From Playlist**.

Customising the interface

When you're settled into a long Internet or work session and have your music playing in the background, chances are you won't want the full Rhythmbox window with all of its bells and whistles taking up space on the screen. Fortunately, there's a trimmed-down version of the interface that you can activate via the menu: click View > Small Display (or press Ctrl+d) and the window will shrink down to a smaller incarnation:

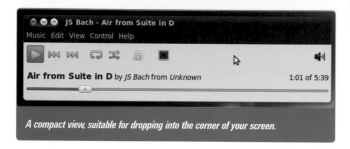

A compact view, suitable for dropping into the corner of your screen.

Go to View > Small Display again to revert back to the normal view. If you're a bit short on screen space and would rather keep Rhythmbox minimised completely, you can still manipulate it using an icon in the system tray. It's the white rectangle with a circle and two buttons, reminiscent of an old-style iPod. Click it while Rhythmbox is playing a song and a menu will appear:

With this you can quickly flick backwards and forwards between tracks without having to fiddle around in the full player window.

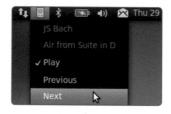

One final thing while we're in Rhythmbox – a rather trivial thing, but fun nonetheless: when you're playing a piece of music, click View > Visualisation from the menu to display some rather snazzy graphical effects to accompany your tunes:

Visualisation doesn't do much to improve your enjoyment of a piece of music, but it lets you set up your Linux box as an attractive-looking jukebox.

Click the drop-down lists underneath the animation to choose different types of effects, and whether to view them embedded into the main window or in full-screen mode.

Rhythmbox preferences

Rhythmbox is a highly configurable music player, as you can see from the options screen (shown below). Click Edit > Preferences from the menu and this window will appear:

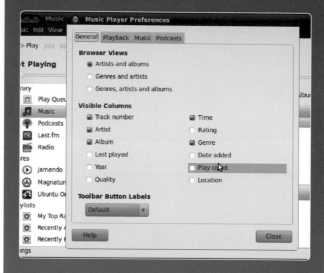

Some of the options worth experimenting with are:

- **Browser Views** – If you prefer sorting your music by albums, choose the first option; alternatively, you can navigate through your tunes based on genre (or a combination of both).

- **Visible columns** – Helpfully, this has an option to enable a Last Played column, which shows up in the song list to tell you when you last heard a piece of music. This is good for two things: it can remind you of music that you've not come across in a while, or show you songs that you're clearly no longer interested in – and can remove to save space!

- **Playback tab, Crossfade** – Want a smooth transition between songs, with the volume being lowered in one while rising in the other? Enable this via the checkbox here. Good for parties and social events when you want a constant, uninterrupted stream of music playing.

- **Music tab, Library Location** – Here you can determine where the application stores your songs. For most systems the default is fine (in your home directory), but if you're on, say, a netbook with limited flash storage and you'd like to keep your tunes on an SD card, look here.

Ripping music from CDs

Let's move on to the job of grabbing music from other sources. If you've bought music online then chances are it will be in MP3 format, and providing there's no DRM (Digital Rights Management) involved, you will be able to simply drop the files into Rhythmbox and play them as described. (If your favourite music service only offers DRM-encrypted versions of music, you'll have to ask them to make it available in a proper, open format or at least release a player for Linux.)

What about audio CDs? To convert these into a format suitable for playing in Rhythmbox, we need to install a program called Sound Juicer.

1 Get Sound Juicer

Click Applications > Ubuntu Software Centre from the main desktop menu, and then search for 'juice'. You'll see that the 'Audio CD Extractor' program appears in the results:

Click Install and the program will be retrieved from the Internet. When the process has finished, click Applications > Sound & Video > Audio CD Extractor from the main desktop menu to start the program.

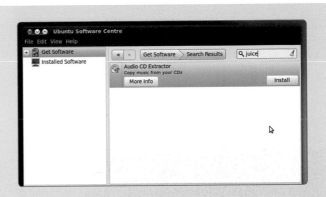

2 Load your CD

The main window will appear. Insert an audio CD and Sound Juicer will scan the disk, looking for the tracks. (If it doesn't do this automatically, click the Disc menu and choose the Re-read Disc option). If you're not connected to the Internet, you'll end up with a list of track numbers and their durations; if you are connected, however, Sound Juicer will access an online database and try to discover more information about the disc, such as the name, artist and names of individual tracks. You should end up with a screen similar to this:

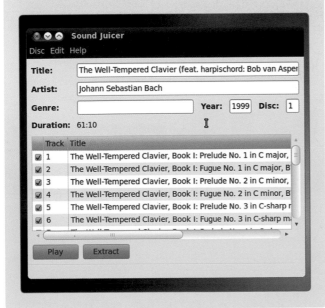

3 Rip the tracks

You can now click a track in the list and then the Play button to listen to it, or the Extract button to generate a file from it. To extract the entire disc to audio files, click Disc > Extract from the menu.

This may take a while, depending on the size of the disc and tracks, but there's a progress bar at the bottom along with an indication of how much time remains. When the process is completed, you'll find a new folder in your home folder containing the tracks – this will be the name of the disc if it could be retrieved from the Internet at the start; if you have no Internet connection, it will be called Unknown Artist.

⚠ Ripping to other file formats

By default, Sound Juicer extracts music into Ogg Vorbis (.ogg) format, a free and open audio file format that can play in Rhythmbox. However, not all personal music players (such as iPods) support Ogg, in which case you will want to extract to MP3 instead. Click Edit > Preferences in the Sound Juicer menu and at the bottom, in the Output Format list, choose the MP3 option. Now, when you extract the disc, you'll see .mp3 files instead of .ogg.

(Note: MP3 support will only appear in the list if you went through the earlier steps of opening an MP3 in Rhythmbox and downloading the codec plugins from the Internet. If you don't see it in the list, go back and perform those steps. To install the plugins manually, click Applications > Ubuntu Software Centre from the desktop menu, then search for 'plugins-ugly' and install the 'GStreamer extra plug-ins' package from the list that appears.)

⚠ Working with MP3 players

Let's look at transferring music to MP3 players. Most of these devices are simple plug-and-play affairs that behave just like regular USB flash storage drives. Plug it in and an icon will appear on the desktop; double-click the icon and you can browse the files in the file manager. (As an option, you may be prompted to open the device in Rhythmbox, in which case you can copy over songs from your playlists.)

But in the simple file manager view, just drag and drop songs into the player, then right-click the desktop icon and choose Safely Remove Device. Now, when you power up the MP3 player, you'll be able to play the new songs that you dragged over.

However, there's another class of portable music player – an especially large class – that works in a different way. Apple's iPod line, along with the iPhone, cannot normally be accessed like a USB flash drive, so there's no simple dragging-and-dropping of files. Instead it has to be accessed through Rhythmbox, but fortunately that's not hard to work with as we've seen before.

For instance, here we've connected an Apple iPhone to our Linux machine. First of all, a dialog box appears asking if we want to transfer photos; after dismissing that we see this:

Inside Rhythmbox we can see the iPhone device in the left-hand panel, along with the playlists on it:

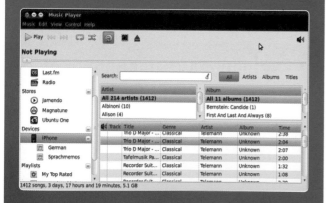

Now we can manage music just as described earlier, dragging tracks between the local music library and the iPhone, dropping tracks into playlists and so forth. After certain operations, you'll see a 'Syncing. . .' message on the screen of your device – never pull the cable out while it's doing this!

If you have music on your iPod or iPhone that you downloaded from the iTunes store, it will be in AAC format and not playable in the standard Rhythmbox installation. Double-click on such a track and Ubuntu will offer to find a suitable codec plugin on the Internet:

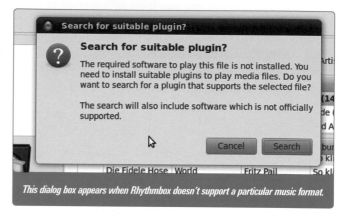

This dialog box appears when Rhythmbox doesn't support a particular music format.

After it has downloaded and installed the plugins, double-click the song again, and this time it should play correctly:

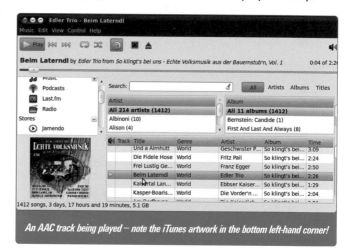

An AAC track being played – note the iTunes artwork in the bottom left-hand corner!

When you've done all the file operations you need, click the Eject button on the toolbar:

Click eject before unplugging your iPod/iPhone so that all changes are synched with the device.

If you need any help with Rhythmbox, it's supplied with very extensive documentation. Click Help > Contents from the menu (or press F1) and you'll see a list of help categories covering all aspects of the program. Alternatively, enter a search term in the box at the top of the window to narrow down information on a particular topic, such as playlists.

MULTIMEDIA
Videos: Totem and VLC

Whereas digital music is largely confined to the MP3, AAC and Ogg Vorbis formats, videos are available in a bewildering range of different types, some of which are very well supported on Linux and some of which aren't. To complicate matters further, some media formats are actually containers for other formats. For instance, a file ending in .avi could actually have MPEG video inside it, or H.264, or one of many other formats. Even the most tech-savvy video fans find the situation almost impossibly hard to fathom out.

Ultimately, then, the best way to find out if a particular video works on Linux is to try to open it. For the moment we're going to stick with the video player that's supplied with Ubuntu, called Totem, but later on we'll look at an alternative player that's not so deeply integrated with the desktop but handles a vast range of video formats with ease.

1 Find your movie
To start, locate the video file that you want to view and double-click on it. In this example we're using an MPEG video called delta.mpg.

The Totem movie player will start up.

2 Getting the right plugins
Depending on the format of the video, Ubuntu might not support it in its default configuration, in which case it will offer to search the Internet for appropriate plugins:

Click Search and Ubuntu will scan its software repositories on the Internet and present you with a list of options:

It's a good idea to leave all options checked – you can't go wrong by having too many media plugins on the system. (As mentioned earlier, these can only be provided via the Internet because certain media codecs have software patents issues in some countries, and the Ubuntu team doesn't want to put these on the main disc.)

3 Retrieve the packages
You may be prompted for your password, and the packages will be retrieved:

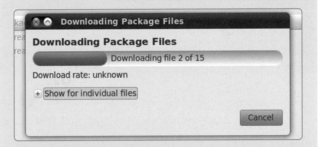

When download has finished, you'll be returned to the main Totem screen and the video will start playing:

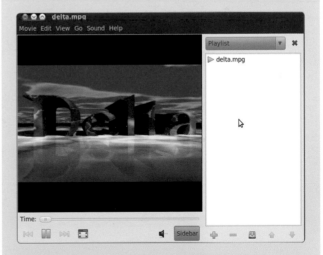

As you try to load different types of video you may be asked to go through a similar process, but ultimately you will end up with a set of video codecs that should cover most of the files that you'll ever come across.

Navigating Totem's interface

Totem is quite a simplistic movie player, and that's a good thing – it has a clean, clutter-free interface and doesn't get in your way with unnecessary bells and whistles. On the right-hand side is a playlist panel, into which you can drag video files from the desktop. Above the playlist is a drop-down box that lets you view the properties of a file, such as the author, date of creation, dimensions, frame rate and so forth.

Totem's main interface.

If you want to get rid of the buttons and panels surrounding the video and just see the video itself, click View > Show Controls from the menu (or press Ctrl+h). The interface will switch to a more minimal mode:

Viewing a video without the controls.

Right-click and choose Show Controls (or press Ctrl+h again) to switch back to the normal view. For a more cinema-like experience you'll want to remove everything from the screen and just see the video, so go to Video > Fullscreen in the menu and press F11. You can then press F11 or Escape to return back to the normal viewing mode.

An alternative: VideoLAN Client

Totem does an excellent job for watching most movies, but it can only do so much. A more advanced tool that supports more formats, including watching DVDs, is VideoLAN Client (aka VLC).

1 Install it

To install this application, click Applications > Ubuntu Software Centre from the desktop menu and enter 'vlc' into the top-right search box:

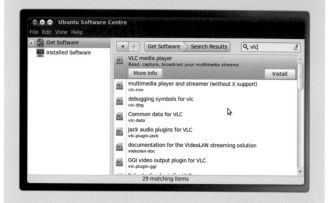

In the first item in the list, 'VLC media player', click the Install button and the packages will be retrieved from the Internet (you may be asked for your password). Once it is installed, you'll find it in the desktop menu under Applications > Sound & Video > VLC media player.

2 Check privacy settings

VLC is a free and open source program, and in contrast to many of the commercial media players it takes privacy very seriously. The first screen you'll see is a note that VLC can, if you want it to, try to find album art for CDs – but it does not collect any data whatsoever. Even the default option is 'Manual download only', erring on the side of caution.

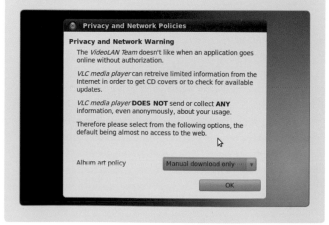

3 The main interface

Anyway, click OK to dismiss this and you'll see the main VLC interface:

Now insert a video DVD. A box may pop up asking which program you want to open it in – just click the close button to get rid of it. Back in VLC, click Media > Open Disc from the menu and choose the DVD option:

As you can see, you can also view VCD discs, which are less common than DVDs but occasionally you might come across them.

4 Playing the disc

Click Play and the movie will begin playing:

Along the bottom of the window you'll see a series of small control buttons. The icons will give you an indication of what most of them do, but otherwise hover the mouse pointer over them for tooltips. To the right is a volume slider that actually lets you go beyond 100%, thereby amplifying the sound of the video.

VideoLAN options

Click the Playback menu and then the Navigation menu to move around in the different sections of the DVD, and see the Video menu to enable subtitles, change the scaling and modify other options. Under the Video menu you'll also find the full-screen mode; press Escape when you've finished watching your film and want to go back to the regular interface.

VLC is such an advanced media player that the options screen (under Tools > Preferences in the menu) has two view modes: simple and all. In most cases you won't need to modify any of the settings here – the defaults are more than good enough for general video watching. Still, if you end up spending a lot of time in VLC it's well worth exploring the range

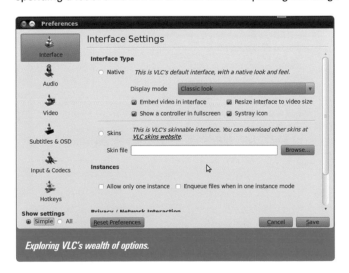

Exploring VLC's wealth of options.

of settings on offer, especially the keybindings under the Hotkeys category; you can alter the way you interact with the player without having to keep reaching over for the mouse.

In the 'All' settings view, underneath the Demuxers expandable list, you can see a list of the video formats that VLC supports, along with settings for each individual format. If VLC is generally working well for you, but ends up hiccuping with certain file types, have a look at options that you can fine-tune.

Installing RealPlayer

Most websites use Flash for streaming audio and video (Flash installation is covered in Section 3), but some use the RealMedia format, as supported by RealPlayer. Helpfully, RealNetworks has created a dedicated player for Linux, which you can access at www.real.com/realplayer/linux:

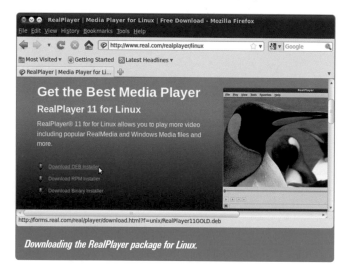

Downloading the RealPlayer package for Linux.

Click on the link that says 'Download DEB installer' – or, if the page has changed by the time you read this, look for a link that downloads a file ending in .deb (you'll see the filename in the status bar at the bottom when you hover over a link). Firefox will offer to open it or save it:

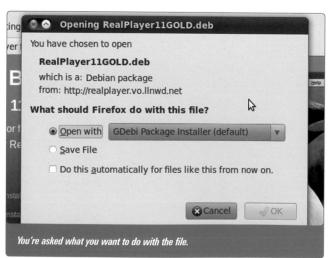

You're asked what you want to do with the file.

RealPlayer has lost out to Flash in the popularity race, but it is still used for many online video streams.

Choose the first option, Open with GDebi Package Installer, and click OK. Once the file has downloaded, the package installer will launch and confirm that you want to go ahead; click the Install Package button. You may be prompted for your password. Once the installation has completed you'll find the program under the Applications > Sound & Video menu as RealPlayer 11.

When you first run RealPlayer, you'll be asked to work through a wizard that tests your connection speed so that you get the best possible video quality. Then you'll arrive at the main RealPlayer window. You can click File > Open File to access a RealMedia file stored locally on your hard drive, or File > Open Location to access a remote stream.

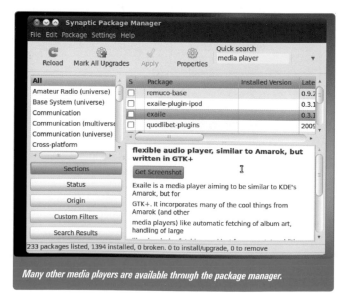

Many other media players are available through the package manager.

MULTIMEDIA
Photos: F-spot

Thanks to the ubiquity of low-cost, good-quality digital cameras, the days of film-based photo processing are virtually at an end. Even better, we can fix problems with our photos before the printing process, and Linux is very well equipped with software to make your snaps look perfect. There's nothing extra to buy, no hidden costs – your Ubuntu installation can do virtually everything you need straight away.

Firstly, let's consider the ways to transfer photos from a camera to your desktop. Most cameras use flash memory cards such as SD or CompactFlash (CF), but you'll need a suitable port on your PC to transfer files this way. Many laptops (and even some PCs) have SD card readers built in now, but failing that you can buy USB readers that accept a variety of cards for a very cheap price – under ten pounds or dollars.

Another way is to simply connect your camera directly to your PC using the USB cable. Here we're connecting a Samsung Digimax camera to the Ubuntu machine, but the process will be essentially identical for your camera too.

1 Connect the camera

After connecting the camera and hitting its power button, Ubuntu will scan the device and see what kind of files it finds on it. You should see this window:

In this case, the default option of 'Open F-Spot' is what you want: F-Spot is the photo manager and editor included with Ubuntu. (For future reference: if you just want to browse the files on the camera directly, like any other storage device, choose Open Folder from the drop-down list. And to launch F-Spot manually, it's in the Applications > Graphics desktop menu.)

2 Import into F-Spot

Next, F-Spot will import the photos from the camera into its library:

Depending on the resolution of your camera (which affects the file size) and the amount of photos that you have, this could take a few minutes. Still, you can scroll around in the top-left panel to remind yourself of the photos that you've taken, and click one to view it in the larger panel on the right.

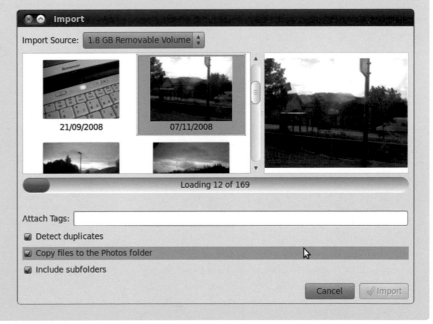

3 F-Spot's interface

Once the progress bar has completed, click Import to confirm that you want to import the pictures, and then you'll arrive at the main F-Spot screen:

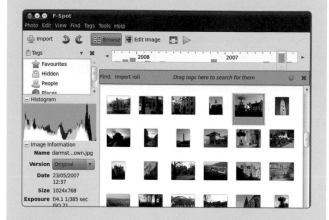

Click on an image to view information about it in the bottom-left panel, such as its size (in pixels) and the date on which it was taken. Above the image thumbnails is a slider that you can drag around to view photos taken in a certain timeframe.

4 Get a detailed view

To view a picture in more detail, simply double-click it to switch to this view:

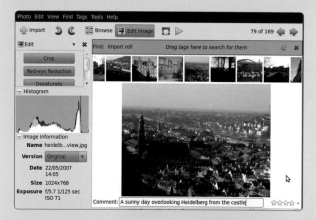

Here's where we can start to explore the photo management features. Beneath the photo is a text box into which you can type a short comment about the picture – eg where it was taken or something memorable about that day. To the right of the comment box is a series of dots; click on these to rate the picture from one to five stars. Underneath the star ratings is a slider for zooming in and out of the image.

5 Rotate an image

Many cameras store the orientation of a photo inside the picture file itself, but if this isn't the case with your pictures you might find some of them looking very odd. However, rotating a photo to the correct orientation only takes a few clicks – use the orange icons in the toolbar towards the top of the window:

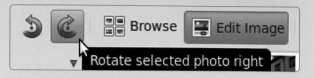

6 Sort with tags

The best way to sort photos is using tags. These are short words that describe the category to which a photo belongs. For instance, in your photo collection you might have photos from both work and your family, in which case you'd want to tag them accordingly to keep them separate. Or perhaps you want to tag some photos that have people in, and other photos that are just scenery.

Right-click on a picture and, in the menu that appears, go to the Attach Tag submenu. There you'll see a list of predefined tags that you can apply to the image: Favourites, People, Places and so forth. Click a tag to attach it, or go to the Remove Tag submenu to remove it:

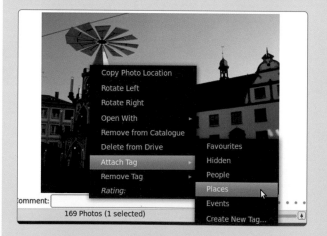

You will probably find the current set of tags too limiting, so under the Attach Tag submenu choose Create New Tag to make a new one. You can even create a tag that has a parent tag – in other words, it's a subset of the parent tag, and choosing that parent tag will display all photos of the subset tags.

Editing facilities

So that's photo management covered: you can now import files from your camera, navigate through them, view information about them, correct any orientation problems and sort them into categories with tags. If you want to import more photos from your camera, or import images from any generic folder on your hard drive, click the Import icon in the top-left of the main F-Spot window. To remove a photo from your collection, simply right-click its thumbnail and choose Remove from Catalogue.

Let's move on to image editing. F-Spot doesn't try to be an all-singing, all-dancing graphics powerhouse like Photoshop, but it does provide the image manipulation essentials that we all need, in a very user-friendly interface.

So, how do you go about narrowing down photos to specific tags? First, return to the thumbnail view by double-clicking on the photo or clicking the Browse button in the toolbar at the top. Then right-click on a few photos and give them tags – in this case, we've applied the Places tag to four pictures:

Four images tagged with Places.

You will see small icons beneath the thumbnails to indicate the tags that they have; in the case of Places, it's an Earth icon. Now look at the top-left panel of the screen, titled Tags. Click and drag a tag into the right-hand Find panel like this:

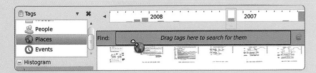

After this, the thumbnail view will only display images that are tagged with the tag you dragged across. Right-click an icon in the Find bar and choose Remove from Search to go back to the previous view.

To see what's available, double-click a picture to bring it into the large view, and then look in the panel at the top-left of the screen, with the heading Edit:

Many of these features require that you select a portion of the image first. For instance, the top option, Crop, requires that you select a specific chunk of the picture, and the remainder is thrown away. Click and drag with the left mouse button on the image to select an area:

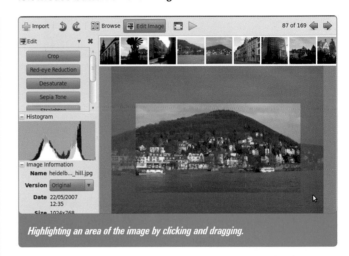

Viewing the image editing options.

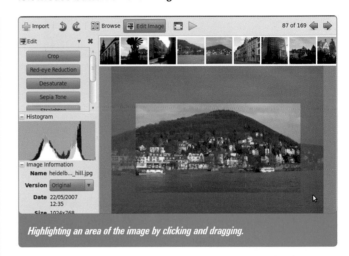

Highlighting an area of the image by clicking and dragging.

Now click the Crop button in the top-left panel and the unselected areas of the picture will be removed:

Next up in the Edit pane is Red-eye Reduction. This is a common annoyance when you're taking photos using a flash – your subject's eyes turn into an entertainingly evil-looking shade of red due to the reflection. F-Spot can try to eliminate this: click and drag to select a small area over the subject's eyes, and then click the Red-eye Reduction button.

Desaturate, meanwhile, removes colour from an image, while Sepia Tone makes your photo look like a classic snap from the olden days:

The bits we didn't want are no longer there.

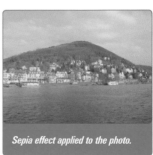

Sepia effect applied to the photo.

The Straighten option lets you rotate images, while still keeping them in the rectangle or square of the original image. If you've taken a photo where the horizon is skewed, or perhaps you want a deliberate slant in your pictures, choose this option and use the slider to change the angle:

Altering the angle of a picture with the Straighten option.

⚠ Exporting to the Internet

Once you've crafted your photo collection to perfection, no doubt you'll want to share it with the world. Thankfully, F-Spot's exporting facilities are excellent. In the main thumbnail view, click Edit > Select All to select every picture. Then click the Photo menu and look inside the Export submenu: you'll see the various services on offer. F-Spot can upload pictures to Flickr, PicasaWeb, SmugMug and Zooomr – in each case, you'll need your username and password to log in.

If you've never heard of these services before, they are online picture-sharing communities. You upload images and other users can comment on them. Flickr and PicasaWeb are two of the most popular services; they're free to join and great fun to use. See www.flickr.com and http://picasaweb.google.com for more information.

Then there's Soft Focus, which introduces some blur around the edges of the photo, while Auto Colour attempts to make the picture's colours bolder and more contrasting, and Adjust Colours brings up a set of sliders for manipulating the exposure, saturation, hue, brightness and contrast.

There's one more editing tool that's not part of the top-left box but is instead accessed via the menu: click Edit > Sharpen to bring up a dialog box in which you can customise how strong you want the operation to be. Usefully, there's a magnifying glass you can drag around to preview the results of the changes – the bottom-left semicircle shows how the area will look after clicking OK:

Previewing the effects of a sharpening job – the numbers are too high here.

After experimenting with the various editing tools, you might have a moment of panic when you see no Undo/Redo under the Edit menu. Worry not: F-Spot has an advanced system to track the different versions of your image, each time you apply a new editing operation. In the bottom-left-hand panel, click the Version drop-down list to navigate between different stages of the editing process. If you want to restore the image to its starting state, choose Original:

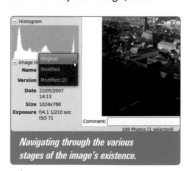

Navigating through the various stages of the image's existence.

Finally, a quick mention of the slide show functionality. You've probably seen digital picture frames in the shops – small LCD screens that display your photos in a cycle, with soft transitions in between. Well, you can turn your Linux box into one of these by clicking View > Slideshow in the F-Spot menu, or by hitting the F5 key. Press Escape to leave the full-screen mode. This is a handy little feature when you have friends round and you'd rather have the computer in the corner displaying something interesting, rather than the usual screensaver.

MULTIMEDIA
Burning discs: Brasero

Making regular backups is one of those things we all say that we should do, but usually we don't do it enough. Yet hard drives are particularly fickle beasts and can stop working at any moment, without warning. Consequently it's a good idea to keep backups of your important data on external media, such as CD-Rs or DVD-Rs. These discs are so cheap now that making weekly backups of vital files isn't a problem.

1 Launch the app

The disc-burning software included with Ubuntu is called Brasero, and it can be found under the Applications > Sound & Video menu. When you launch it for the first time you'll be prompted to create a new project:

2 Start an Audio project

Down the left-hand side you can see the different types of discs you can create. Let's start with Audio project: click its button and a new window will appear with a large, empty area, inviting you to drag files into it. You can now open up the file manager (eg Places > Home Folder from the desktop menu) and start clicking and dragging to copy music files from your hard drive into the new Brasero project:

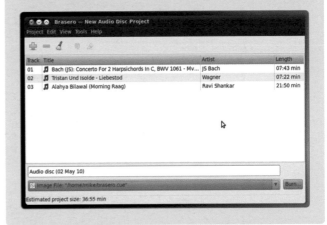

3 Give the disc a name

An alternative route is to click the green plus button in the top-left of the window and then locate music files using the file browser. Either way, you can add music in MP3 or Ogg format, and click and drag track names in the list to reorder them on the disc.

Towards the bottom of the screen you'll see a text box, into which you can type the name of the CD. Then there's a drop-down list for selecting your CD writing device – or, if you just want to write a CD image file for now and burn it later, there's an option for that too. Finally there's a very useful time indicator, showing the total duration of the current project in minutes and seconds. Generally, the safe limit for most CD-R discs is 75 minutes, so we recommend keeping below that to ensure that your disc works on all drives.

4 Burn it!

When you're ready to go, insert a CD-R and hit the Burn button in the bottom-right. The burning process may take a while depending on the duration of your CD and the speed of your CD writer.

Writing data CDs and DVDs

The next option in the Brasero startup screen is Data project – the method for creating backup CDs or DVDs of your files. As with the Audio CD option, this presents you with an empty screen on to which you can drag and drop files and folders from the file manager. This time, however, there's a very useful Space column that shows you which files are taking up the most room:

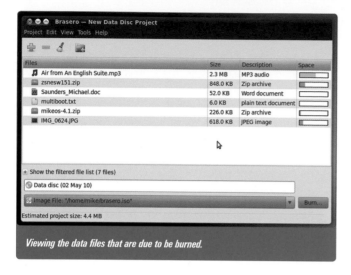

Viewing the data files that are due to be burned.

In this example, in the right-hand column we can see that the .mp3 file at the top is taking up over half of the space in the current project – in other words, it's bigger than all of the other files put together. This is an extremely useful feature when your backup files are bigger than the CD-R or DVD-R you're going to write to, and you need to get rid of something quickly.

It certainly helps when you realise that you can remove a relatively pointless office party video and suddenly have lots of room for important documents! Click an item in the list and press the Del key to remove it. (This won't delete it from your hard drive, but simply remove it from the list of files to be burned.)

It's important to note that Linux and Windows have different limits on the type of filenames that they can use. Linux is the most flexible, and can use very long filenames with a wide variety of characters, but Windows is more restrictive, especially when it comes to reading files from a CD or DVD. Therefore you might occasionally see this dialog box when adding files or folders:

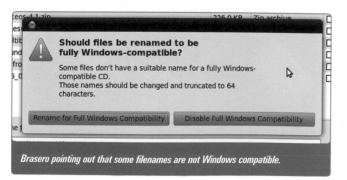

Brasero pointing out that some filenames are not Windows compatible.

Here you have the option to automatically shorten filenames longer than 64 letters/numbers, in which case they'll work properly on Windows systems, or disable Windows compatibility. If the disc you're burning is purely a personal backup that you will only access on your Linux machine, you can safely choose the latter option here.

As with audio CDs, at the bottom of the main window you can set the name of the disc, choose the device you want to use for burning, and get an overall indication of how much space the current project uses. When you're ready to burn, insert your disc. If you have a rewriteable disc – such as a CD-RW or DVD-RW – you can wipe it clean before writing by clicking Tools > Blank. Otherwise just click the Burn button to start the writing process.

Note that if you don't want to burn anything at this point, and you want to come back to this project later, just close the Brasero window. When you next start the program you'll see 'Last Unsaved Project' under the 'Recent projects' panel on the right, so click that button to resume.

Creating video discs

Let's move on to the third option, Video project. Brasero is not an advanced video editing suite by any means, but it's a good, quick way to share home movies with people. However, it needs a few extras from the Internet to ensure that it can work with the widest possible range of video file formats.

1 Get the right codecs

In the desktop menu, click Applications > Ubuntu Software Centre, then enter 'ffmpeg' into the top-right search box:

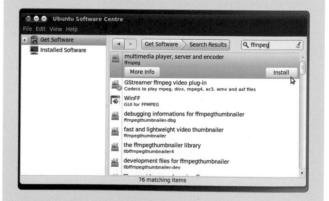

Click Install and the packages will be retrieved from the Internet and installed. Now do the same for 'vcdimager', 'dvdauthor' and 'mjpegtools'. Lastly, search for 'plugins-bad' and install the program that says 'GStreamer plug-ins for aac, xvid, mpeg2, faad'.

2 Fire up Brasero

When you're done, restart Brasero, click the Video project and you'll be presented with a mostly empty window, just like with the previous two options. This time, however, you can only drag video files into it – eg files ending in .mpg or .avi. Note that Brasero also supports Ogg Theora video files, which are based on a totally open and free format, and have the filename extension .ogg or .ogv (to distinguish it from the Ogg Vorbis audio format discussed earlier).

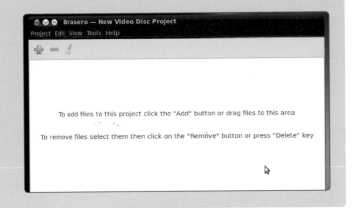

3 Preview your clips

Once you've dragged them into the window, you'll see thumbnails like this. Click on a video file to get a preview of it beneath. When you're happy with your collection, click on the Burn button (or go to Project > Burn in the menu). In the dialog that appears you can choose whether to generate a DVD or SVCD, and set the video format: PAL/SECAM is used in most of Europe, Asia, the Middle East and Australasia, whereas NTSC is used in the USA, Japan, South Korea and some parts of South America. When you're done, you'll have a disc that should be playable in a normal DVD drive – try it in VLC to confirm that it works.

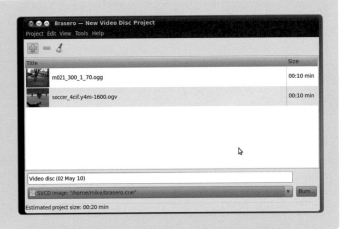

Other Brasero features to explore

The final two options in Brasero's startup screen are for making direct duplicates of CDs or DVDs, and burning an existing disc image to a physical disc. The latter option is especially useful if you start experimenting with other Linux distributions: in most cases, you'll download these from the Internet in ISO format (with an .iso file extension), which means that they're a direct representation of a disc's contents in a single file. You can't just copy it on to a CD-R or DVD-R to make it work – it needs to be written directly with the Burn image option in Brasero.

Advanced video editing is beyond the scope of this book, but we'll point out a program that's full of features and included with Ubuntu as standard: PiTiVi. You'll find this in the Applications > Sound & Video menu on the desktop, and it lets you drag-and-drop clips into a library and then place them into a timeline beneath. You can have separate sources for audio and video, placing clips at different locations, and then render the whole lot together into a new movie. If you're familiar with video editing software then you won't find it hard to grasp; explore the menus to see what it's capable of.

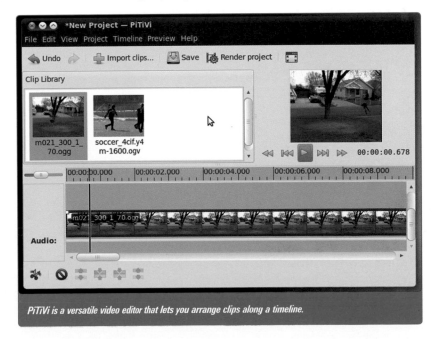

PiTiVi is a versatile video editor that lets you arrange clips along a timeline.

Administration

In this section

ADMINISTRATION
The Linux filesystem

U p until this point, we've just been working in the home directory (aka home folder) – /home/yourusername. Linux is an exceptionally well-designed OS that keeps you out of harm's way, and prevents you from accidentally making changes to critical system files. For typical day-to-day computing you never need to venture outside of your home directory, but when you want to explore deeper into the system and perform administration tasks it's a good idea to know what's going on in the rest of the filesystem.

Unlike Windows, where you have files scattered across multiple drives (C:, D: etc), in Linux there's just one main directory that's the starting point for everything else. This is called the 'root' directory and is a single forward slash: /. The root directory is the deepest point you can go in the filesystem – it is not a subdirectory of anything else. Slashes are used to separate directories in Linux, hence why a single slash on its own is the root, and not part of anything else. For instance, in the root directory you have 'home', which contains users' home folders. This is why the full location for your home folder is:

/home/yourusername

The first slash is the root directory, then you see the home directory, followed by another slash and finally a directory for your username. A Linux installation can have multiple users (we'll cover that later), so you could have /home/mike, /home/bob and so forth. Let's browse around some of the other directories on the filesystem and see what they do. Click Places > Computer from the menu to open the file manager, and then double-click the File System icon:

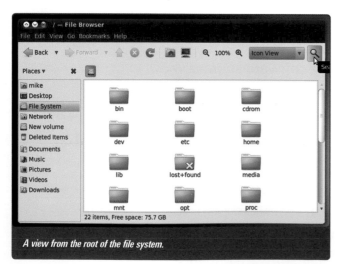

A view from the root of the file system.

In the title of the window you'll see '/', which shows that we're in the root of the filesystem. We can't go any higher up than this, hence why the up arrow in the toolbar is faded out. Here's what the directories do:

■ **/bin** – Contains binary files – ie executable programs. These are not graphical applications such as Firefox, and won't do anything if you double-click them. They are command-line utilities that can be run by any user, as described in more detail in Section 7.

■ **/boot** – Contains files used for booting the system. In here you'll see a file that begins with 'vmlinuz' – this is the kernel, the absolute core of the operating system. The kernel is loaded by the GRUB bootloader (see inside the 'grub' folder and the 'grub.cfg' text file) when the system starts. From there the kernel manages memory, loads hardware drivers, multitasks your programs and so forth.

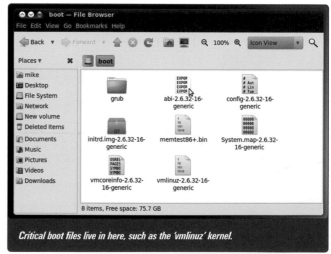

Critical boot files live in here, such as the 'vmlinuz' kernel.

■ **/cdrom** – This will contain the contents of a CD or DVD when you've inserted one.

■ **/dev** – System devices. In Linux (and Unix) almost everything on the system is represented as a file. For instance, /dev/sda could be the file that points to your hard drive – if you were to write data to that file, it would write it directly to your disk! /dev/random is a random number generator; /dev/input/mouse0 is your mouse.

/dev contains subdirectories for disks, input devices, network devices and many others.

- **/etc** – System-wide configuration files. These are mainly text files and contain options for users, security, power management, networking and other aspects of the system. Some applications place their default settings here too after installation.

Most /etc configuration files are in plain text, so you can double-click them to view them.

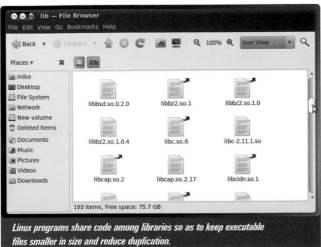

Linux programs share code among libraries so as to keep executable files smaller in size and reduce duplication.

- **/home** – Contains home directories as described earlier.

- **/lib** – System libraries. These are compilations of executable code that any program can use. For instance, every program written in the C language needs to use features provided by the C library: if all programs had to include it in their own executable files, there'd be a lot of duplication and waste. Consequently libraries are shared here. The C library that almost every program uses is libc.so.6 (the arrow on the icon means that it's a link, or short cut, to another file).

- **/lost+found** – Files are dropped here if the system loses power and restarts abruptly. Linux will perform a disk check; if it finds any bits of data that weren't saved properly before the power loss, it will drop them here. The cross on the folder means that only the root (admin) user can access it (see 'Editing and saving' in Section 7).

- **/media** – The place where external drives appear after they're inserted. For instance, plug in a USB key and a folder will appear here with its name so that you can browse it.

- **/mnt** – Mount points, where you can attach drives and network resources. It has largely been replaced by /media now.

- **/opt** – Optional software. Some large programs place their files in subdirectories in here.

- **/proc** – Process information. When you run programs, they create subdirectories in here containing information on their status – eg usage of memory and other files. Graphical system management tools can read and parse these files to present a more human-understandable facade.

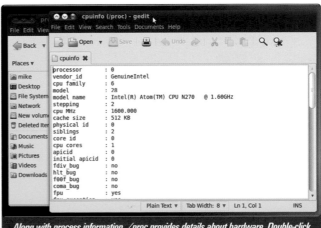

Along with process information, /proc provides details about hardware. Double-click the 'cpuinfo' file to see what capabilities your CPU has.

- **/root** – Files for the 'root' (admin) user; this is not related to the root directory. Because only the root user can access this, it's locked out. Unless you perform any actions as the root user, though, nothing happens in here.

- **/sbin** – Superuser binaries – that is, executable programs that can only be run as the 'root' admin user.

- **/selinux** – Files to handle one of Linux's security frameworks.

- **/srv** – Can be used by server software such as Apache (covered in Section 7).

- **/sys** – Provides access to system information. As with /dev, because everything in Linux is represented as a file, here you can access information on the kernel and devices (/dev contains links to the actual devices themselves). Most of these files are very cryptic, but graphical tools can load these files, parse them and show the results in a more friendly fashion.

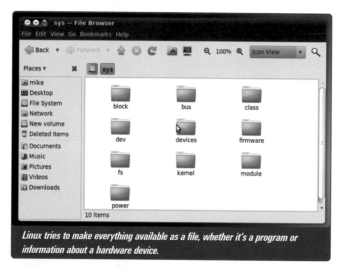

Linux tries to make everything available as a file, whether it's a program or information about a hardware device.

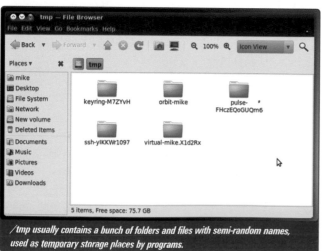

/tmp usually contains a bunch of folders and files with semi-random names, used as temporary storage places by programs.

- **/tmp** – Temporary files used by applications. This is normally purged when the system boots.

- **/usr** – Non-system files – that is, mostly graphical programs and libraries. Whereas /bin and /lib contain important base files to be used at the command line, in /usr/bin you'll find desktop software, and in /usr/lib you'll find libraries and files for those programs. (Some command line programs that aren't part of the base system place files here too.) For instance, go into /usr/bin and double-click the 'gedit' icon to start the text editor.

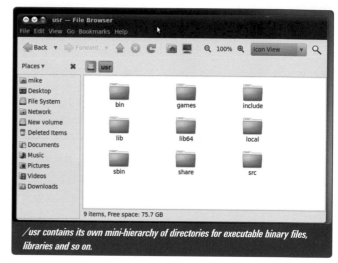

/usr contains its own mini-hierarchy of directories for executable binary files, libraries and so on.

- **/var** – Varying files – files that change a lot, such as logs and databases – live here.

In your typical day-to-day Linux use you won't need to poke around inside these directories, but it's worth knowing exactly what they do for future reference. When you're fixing a damaged installation or need to perform an advanced task, you can delve into these folders without worries!

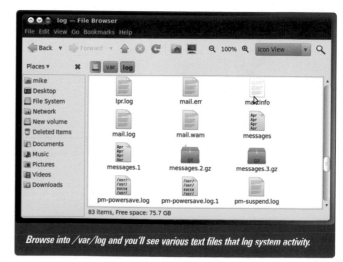

Browse into /var/log and you'll see various text files that log system activity.

ADMINISTRATION
Managing hardware

One of the major differences between Linux and other operating systems like Windows is how hardware is managed. In Windows, when you buy a new piece of hardware you're typically given a driver disc which then installs various files into random places on your computer, and you cross your fingers and hope for the best. In Linux, drivers are supplied with the operating system itself, and are developed in conjunction with the whole OS.

As a result, very rarely will you see standalone Linux drivers – the developers want as much as possible to work 'out of the box'. Sometimes, as in the case of video cards, there are two drivers: one which is built into the operating system and works straight away, and another, proprietary version from the maker of the graphics chip, which adds more features. Because Ubuntu champions the open source and free software movements, and values free (sharable and modifiable) software extremely highly, the built-in versions of drivers are used by default.

1 View available drivers
However, you can find out what proprietary drivers are available by clicking System > Administration > Hardware Drivers from the menu. This window will appear:

In our case, we're on a machine that has a Broadcom wireless chip, and Ubuntu has found a proprietary driver that we can use. Note the warning at the top: when you're using proprietary drivers you're using software that's not developed as part of the Linux project, and therefore you can't be guaranteed that the driver will be supported forever. This is one of the reasons why Linux distribution makers prefer open source drivers – they can be developed and updated for as long as is required.

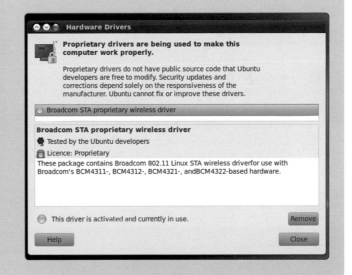

2 Adding a new piece of hardware
When you add a piece of hardware, it should be detected and activated automatically. For instance, if you plug in a printer you should see a new icon in the system tray (top right) on the screen, along with a pop-up message that your printer has been found and activated. If it isn't automatically detected or you want to use a printer on the network, click System > Administration > Printing to open the printer configuration screen. Then click Add and choose the printer from the list of devices or from the location on the network.

3 Configuring a printer
After this, you can configure the settings of your printer by selecting it in the list and going to Printer > Properties. You can then change the paper size, printing mode and other options. If you still have problems, visit www.openprinting.org – this site has a printer compatibility database, so you can find out how well your specific printer is supported in Linux. Many printers are based on other models in the range, so quite often you can use a driver for a different model and it will work just as well.

Managing external storage devices

For storage devices, such as external hard drives and USB flash memory keys, these will appear as soon as you plug them in:

After plugging in an external storage device, its contents will appear in the file manager.

You can also access the device via its icon on the desktop or via the Places menu at the top of the screen. Note that it's not a good idea to quickly remove a drive after you've written data to it: the kernel stores up data in a buffer and then writes lots out in one large lump for performance reasons. If you copy a file into a device and then remove it straight away, the file may not have been copied fully – or at all. To make sure that all data is written before you remove the device, right-click on its icon on the desktop and choose Safely Remove Drive.

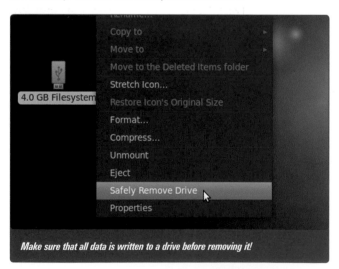

Make sure that all data is written to a drive before removing it!

Some devices won't provide any immediate visual feedback when inserted. A USB joypad or joystick, for instance, doesn't require any configuration so nothing will appear when you plug it in. That said, sometimes you may want to confirm that a device has been detected correctly, or find out what the kernel thinks it is. There's a quick way to do this.

⚠ Detecting a device

Click Applications > Accessories > Terminal to open a command line window, and then type in 'dmesg' and press Enter. Lots of system information text will scroll by, taken from the system log, most of which may look like gibberish. However, towards the bottom you will see information about the device you've just plugged in:

In this instance, we inserted a USB joypad before running 'dmesg', and here we've highlighted the relevant information from the log. We can see that a 'new low speed USB device' was inserted into the system, and it was determined as an 'input' device called 'Gamepad [Mega World]'. So, the kernel has successfully recognised that we have inserted a device, and it has correctly identified it as a game controller.

Using 'dmesg' is an excellent way to find out what's going on when you add and remove devices, and it's especially useful if you're having trouble getting a particular piece of hardware to work. If you're posting a help request on a Linux website forum (see 'Online resources for help' in the Appendices) then it's a good idea to copy and paste the relevant bits of text from the output of 'dmesg' into the question. If you're not sure what's relevant, copy and paste the last screen-load of text. With this information, other Linux users who've figured out how to get the device working will be able to point you in the right direction.

```
[12992.498413] usbcore: registered new interface driver usbhid
[12992.500704] usbhid: v2.6:USB HID core driver
[13625.536250] usb 2-1: USB disconnect, address 2
mike@mike-laptop:~$
```

Viewing log files

Another way to view the output of 'dmesg', and the contents of other system log files, is by using the graphical tool under System > Administration > Log File Viewer. When it starts up you'll see this window:

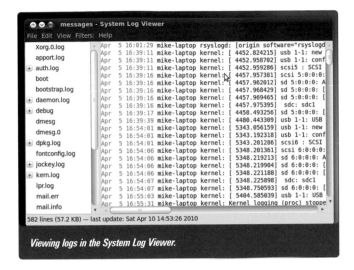

Viewing logs in the System Log Viewer.

Down the left-hand side you'll see a list of log files that you can click on to display the full log in the panel on the right. Some of the log file names have plus (+) boxes next to them; click these to view logs from previous days. The function of some of these log files is described in depth in Section 7, 'Editing and saving', but here are some quick pointers for now:

- **Xorg.0.log** – For the video subsystem. Look at this if you have problems with your graphics.

- **auth.log** – Shows login attempts, both successful and unsuccessful.

- **daemon.log** – Background processes, such as network configuration utilities, post entries in this file.

- **dmesg** – The kernel log as described earlier. Look here for hardware messages.

- **dpkg.log** – Contains information about software package installations and removals.

- **messages** – General informational messages about the state of the system.

- **syslog** – Applications post status messages here.

- **user.log** – Messages from applications started by a regular user, rather than by the system.

A bit of historical Unix baggage comes into play here and there's certainly quite a lot of overlap between the log files, but it's a good idea to know what they do and where to look if something goes wrong. Because some of the log files are very long, the viewer lets you create filters which narrow down the entries displayed. Click Filters > Manage Filters from the menu, and then the Add button to create a new filter.

Let's say you want to only view the log entries that contain the word 'USB'. Give your filter a name (eg 'Only USB') and then type 'USB' into the Regular Expression box. Next, choose Highlight from the options and select the foreground and background colours that you want to apply to the results. Your screen should end up looking something like this:

Setting filter options.

Click Apply and go back to the main Log Viewer window. Click the Filters menu and check the box next to your new filter, Only USB. Now choose a log file and scroll around, and you'll see that lines containing 'USB' are matched and highlighted accordingly:

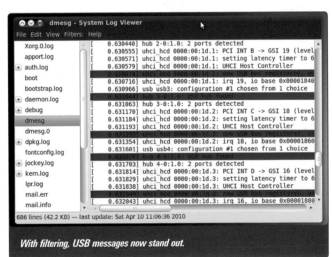

With filtering, USB messages now stand out.

If you only want to view lines that contain 'USB', click the Filters menu and check the Show matches only box.

Monitoring the system

A healthy system requires that no single program is eating up all of your CPU, memory or hard drive resources. Due to Linux's famed reliability, a single program can't normally take down the whole system (unless it is given direct hardware access, which is very rare!) so you don't have to keep fiddling with a task manager like in the bad old Windows days. Nonetheless, Ubuntu includes a useful tool for monitoring the system and killing any program that gets out of hand.

1 Start the System Monitor

Click System > Administration > System Monitor and you'll see a screen like this:

Along the top you'll see four tabs: System, Processes, Resources and File Systems.

2 View processes

Click into Processes and you'll see a list of programs running on the system:

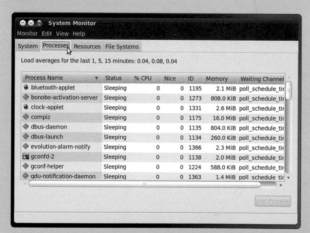

Many of these are system processes – you won't have seen them in the Applications menu before. In most cases a process is the same as a program, but some large pieces of software can spawn multiple processes. You can sort the list of processes by clicking on the columns along the top of the table; for instance, if you want to see what's using the most CPU power, click on the '% CPU' column so that it has an upward-pointing arrow next to it.

3 Kill an errant process

It's usually very obvious if there's a problem with a program. If it's constantly using over 95% of CPU and is not responding to your input, then chances are it has crashed. Click the process in the list and then the End Process button. You will be prompted to confirm the termination operation:

End Process attempts to send a friendly 'please shut down now' request to a process. If that doesn't work, the process has totally spiralled out of control and needs something heavier, so click the process and then Edit > Kill Process from the menu.

4 View resource usage

Meanwhile, the Resources tab is a great way to get an overview of CPU, memory and network activity:

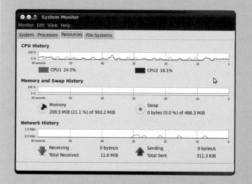

Viewing system activity in graph format.

Each resource is accompanied by a constantly updating graph, giving you an at-a-glance view of resource usage. Note that in the memory section, swap refers to virtual memory – ie the partition on the hard drive to which real RAM is 'swapped out' when it hasn't been used for a while.

5 Configure the appearance

Finally there's the File Systems tab that shows disk usage across your partition(s). The System Monitor is quite configurable: click Edit > Preferences and you can add more information to the display, eg the user that started each process or the time at which it was started.

ADMINISTRATION
User accounts

User accounts are central to the Linux and Unix philosophy of system security. Everyone must have some sort of identity. During the installation process you created a username and password so that you could log in to the system; this is the user account you're currently using. By default there's another, special, user account set up during the installation – that for 'root', or the administrator.

When you perform certain administration tasks or run certain administrator-level programs, especially those under the System > Administration menu, you'll often be asked to enter your password. This confirms that you're the actual user of this machine and you have the authority to make certain changes, so that random people can't just walk up to your PC and start playing around with (and potentially breaking) important system settings! After you've entered your password, the system runs the administration tools as the 'root' user that has the power to manipulate all files

and settings on the system. (Generally, your normal user account can only modify files in your home directory.)

You might, however, want to add another user account to your system. Reasons include:

■ You want a family member or friend to use your machine, but you want them to have their own desktop settings and not have access to your personal files.
■ You're testing something and you want to create a vanilla, out-of-the-box desktop experience.
■ You want to create a 'guest' account that anyone can use – eg if your Linux machine is also functioning as a Linux kiosk – that you can remove and re-add to start afresh.

Each user account has its own home directory, desktop settings and application settings, and one user cannot modify the files of another (only root has the power to do that).

1 Open the user management tool
To add a new user, go to System > Administration > Users and Groups via the desktop menu.

You'll see a screen like this, with 'Mike S' and 'mike' replaced by your own name and username:

2 Add a new account
Click Add on the left-hand side and a dialog box will appear, prompting you to enter a full name for the user:

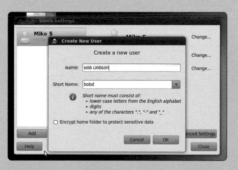

Filling in the details for the new user.

Note that as you type the full name of the user into the first box, the 'Short Name' box is automatically filled with a suggested username. You don't have to accept this – click into the box and edit it if you want something different. Towards the bottom left you'll see a checkbox for encrypting the home folder. On a home PC you generally won't need this, but if you're running Linux on a laptop that you're going to be using in public, it's a good idea to check this box. You'll get a minor performance hit when opening large files, but if you're unlucky and someone steals your laptop they won't have access to your files (unless they know your password).

3 Set a password

When you click OK you may be prompted to enter your password, because you're about to change a system setting. Then you'll be prompted to create the password for the new user account:

You can either invent a password yourself or generate one automatically if you're stuck for ideas. Click OK when you're finished.

4 Test the account

You can now try the user account by clicking on the power icon in the top-right corner of the screen:

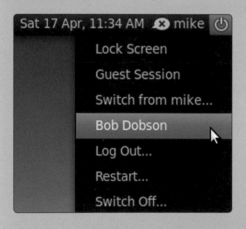

Switching users via the power button.

You can either end the current session by clicking Log Out, and then log in as the new account; or alternatively, you'll see the name of the new user in the menu – clicking it lets you immediately run a desktop as the new user, with your original account still active in the background. You can keep using the power menu to switch between the accounts.

Further user management options

Let's look at some further options. Relaunch the Users and Groups tool, click on a username on the left-hand side and click the Advanced Settings button towards the bottom-right of the window. When the dialog box pops up, select the User Privileges tab and you'll see a display like this:

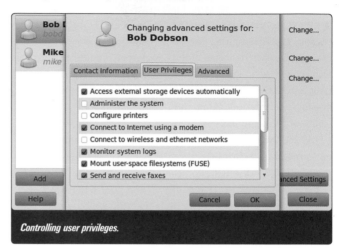

Controlling user privileges.

These options are an excellent way to lock down an account. For instance, perhaps you've created an account for a young child so that he/she can play some educational games and explore the computer. (Perhaps you want to set them on a path to a lucrative programming career!) You probably wouldn't want the child to be on the Internet just yet, so you can block the account from accessing the Internet here.

Or another scenario: you're setting up a Linux machine as an Internet kiosk for your local public library. In this case you do want people to have access to the Internet, but you may want it to be very locked down so that nobody uses it for pirating movies and music. Here you can prevent access to external storage devices, making the machine a pure web-browsing terminal without the complications of file sharing.

To change a user's password, go back to the main Users and Groups window and click 'Change. . .' next to the Password entry on the right:

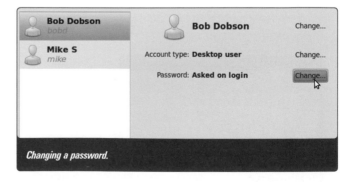

Changing a password.

A password prompt dialog box will appear, the same as the one that we saw when creating the new account.

ADMINISTRATION
Managing software

Back in Section 2 (The desktop) we looked at using the Ubuntu Software Centre to obtain extra programs via the Internet. In most cases the Software Centre does an excellent job exploring and retrieving software, but it is merely a simplified front-end to a very powerful and flexible software management system. Here we're going to look at Synaptic, Ubuntu's advanced software manager – but first, we need to understand how software is distributed in the Linux world.

If you've spent some time with Windows, you'll be familiar with its software distribution method: there isn't one. If you want a program, say a vector graphics editor, you'll do a bit of searching on Google and come across a few sites. If you're lucky, you might find a program that you like, and if you're even luckier, it'll be free of charge. Then you want to make sure that the download is legitimate and not full of viruses – after all, downloading and running random Windows programs off the Internet is a sure-fire recipe for disaster. Even if the program installs and runs correctly, you may not get automatic updates – you'll have to keep checking the program's website for new versions.

Linux is different. In Linux, the makers of the software focus purely on the making – the programming, testing, bugfixing. The distribution methods are handled by the individual Linux distribution. Let's take our vector graphics editor, for instance: Inkscape is the best such tool for Linux. The Inkscape developers

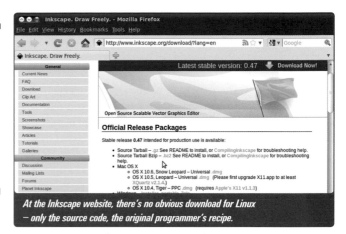

At the Inkscape website, there's no obvious download for Linux – only the source code, the original programmer's recipe.

at www.inkscape.org don't have much in the way of downloads for Linux; only the source code, which needs to be compiled and is a very advanced subject.

However, the Ubuntu (and Debian) developers say: 'Hey, this looks like a great program! We think Debian/Ubuntu users would like it. So let's compile it ourselves, package it up neatly and make it available in the Software Centre. We'll keep updating it with fixes and new versions as they're released.' Consequently, Inkscape is available to us, as Ubuntu users, via the Software Centre without us having to hunt around for it on the net and download random files.

When you launch the Software Centre you're connecting to a bunch of 'repositories' – that is, Ubuntu servers that contain all the files for the programs available. These programs are sent to your machine in packages. Many programs consist of just one package, whereas others are split up to save bandwidth. For instance, the OpenOffice.org suite is huge, but it is split up into separate packages for the word processor, spreadsheet etc components. If a security hole is discovered in the spreadsheet, and the Ubuntu developers make an updated package, your update manager only needs to grab that new package and not the entire suite all over again.

The horror of finding new software for Windows. Trawling through countless messy, advert-laden websites is a tiresome chore.

Understanding Synaptic

Let's explore Synaptic, an advanced software management tool. Launch it via System > Administration > Synaptic Package Manager in the main menu. This screen will appear:

Right from the start you can see that it's a lot busier than the Software Centre, and clearly geared towards administrators. The screen is split into four panes: the top-left, by default, shows all the different categories of software available. Underneath is a series of buttons to change the list above – eg instead of categories you can view packages by their status, or where they come from on the Internet (the Ubuntu repository in which they live). In the top-right you have a list of packages, while underneath that is the description of a package name that you click on.

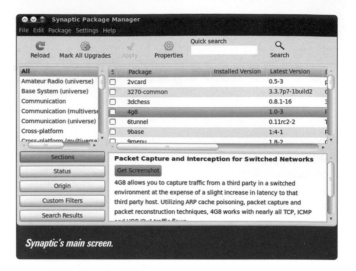

Synaptic's main screen.

1 Mark a package for installation

A package with an empty checkbox next to it means that it's available, but not installed. If it's green then it means that it's already installed:

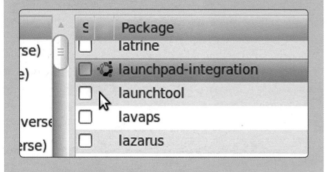

To install a package, right-click on its name in the list and choose Mark for Installation:

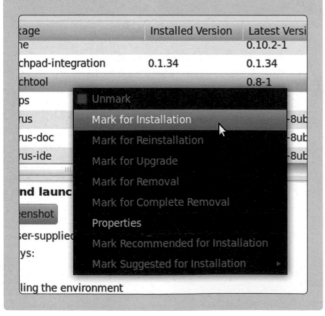

2 Check for dependencies

Synaptic may tell you that it will need to install other packages – 'dependencies' – on which the program relies. Unlike in the Software Centre, the program isn't installed immediately; instead, Synaptic works in a batch mode, where you set up all the options you want before launching a complete install/remove process. You can now go around marking other programs for installation, or right-click on an installed package and mark it for removal. (There's 'removal' and 'complete removal' – the former leaves a program's configuration files on the system, whereas the latter doesn't.)

3 Apply the changes

When you're ready to turn your settings into reality, click the Apply button on the toolbar and Synaptic will explain exactly what it's going to do:

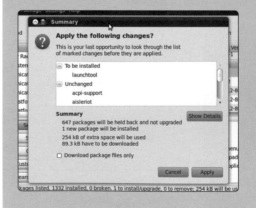

You get plenty of information about the size of the download, number of packages needed, and how much disk space will be used after the operation is complete.

4 Get detailed information

Synaptic also provides a huge amount of information on individual packages. Click an already installed (green box) package in the list, and then the Properties button on the toolbar. You'll see an information panel with its version number, size (in terms of disk space usage) and more:

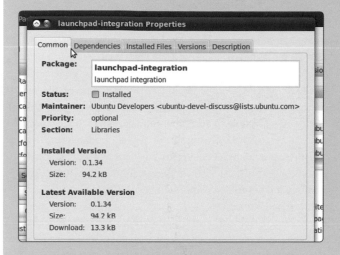

Click the Dependencies tab and you can see the other packages that it needs (labelled 'Depends') or other packages that would work especially well with this one, but aren't required (labelled 'Suggests'):

In the drop-down list under the tabs you can switch the view to 'Dependent packages' – that is, other packages that depend on this one to be installed before they can

be installed. There's also the Installed Files tab, which shows you a detailed list of the contents of the package:

5 Search for more packages

Synaptic also includes searching facilities. There's the 'Quick search' panel at the top of the main window, but if you click the Search button to the right of it you'll see this more in-depth search box:

If you know exactly what you're looking for you can just search by name, but if you're looking for a genre of software (eg image editors) you can also search package descriptions. There are other options as well, for searching dependencies and version numbers.

⚠ What do packages contain?

Packages are interesting beasts, in that they contain a wide range of files, compressed into one neat bundle. You can't just open a package in a text editor and look at the contents – it's a bit more complicated than that. (However, at the command prompt you can enter 'less filename.deb' and it will show you a list of all files inside the package.)

Typically, what you'll find in a package are:

- **Binary files** – These are the machine code, executable files that run the program. Some applications consist of one big binary, others multiple programs that work together.
- **Libraries** – These are also binary, machine code files, but they are not executed on their own. Instead, the main program – and other programs on the machine – can 'link' to them, using their facilities and routines. It's a great way to share resources and reduce duplication.
- **Images** – Toolbar buttons, splash screens and other image files are often included too.
- **Documentation** – Usually as XML, HTML or plain text, this could be a single quick guide or a complete handbook.
- **Installation and removal scripts** – For some advanced, system-level software, certain actions are needed after installation (such as the modification of system startup files). A package can contain scripts that are executed when the package is installed and removed.

Adding new package repositories

As mentioned earlier, repositories are Internet servers that contain packages. By default, Ubuntu is set up to use the repositories provided by the Ubuntu team, which include almost every popular free software program in the universe. In Synaptic, click Settings > Repositories and look at the first tab, Ubuntu Software:

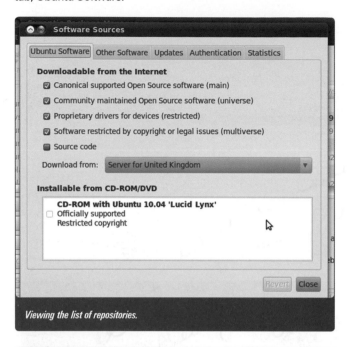

Viewing the list of repositories.

Here you can see the different repositories available to Ubuntu users. The first one, 'main', contains all of the software placed on to your hard drive in a normal Ubuntu installation, along with some extra applications. These are extremely well-maintained packages – full-time, paid developers make sure that they're always up to date and patched with the latest security fixes.

The 'universe' repository includes many thousands of extra programs, but they're supported by the community rather than paid developers, so updates may not arrive as swiftly. Then there are repositories for packages with potential copyright and patent issues – for instance, encrypted DVD playback. Software patents aren't active around the whole world, so whether a package is legally difficult depends on your country, but to be on the safe side the Ubuntu team place such packages in a separate location.

Now, it's possible to add other repositories to the system, so that you can get new programs and regular updates from sources outside of the Ubuntu ecosystem. Take, for instance, Google's Chrome web browser – it's very popular but not included in the default Ubuntu installation or available in the regular Ubuntu repositories.

Here we're going to add Google's repository to our installation so that we can get Chrome, Picasa and other Google apps, along with updates as they become available. (Note that due to the fast-paced nature of the Internet, the following Internet addresses and filenames may be different as you're reading this, so don't copy it as a literal step-by-step process. Take it as an overall guide and adapt it for the repositories that you find on your travels.)

1 Get the repository information
Going to the Google website we see this information for Ubuntu and Debian users:

However, their guide is all based on the command line, whereas we can do this more elegantly in Synaptic. First of all, we need to get a 'package signing key' – a file which verifies that Google's repositories and packages are legitimate and keeps us secure. On Google's page we see that it tells us to download a .pub key from here:

https://dl-ssl.google.com/linux/linux_signing_key.pub

2 Save the repository URL
We copy and paste that URL into the address bar and hit Enter to view it:

We're going to need this information, so click Edit > Select All and then Edit > Copy to save it to the clipboard.

3 Add to Synaptic

Now go back to Synaptic, back into the Settings > Repositories dialog where we were before. Click into the Authentication tab. Beneath the two existing entries in the 'Trusted software providers' list, right-click and choose 'Add key from paste data':

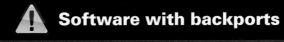

4 Confirm that it works

Google Inc's entry is now in the list, so that Synaptic knows that it's a legitimate source for packages that have been checked and signed off by the Google team:

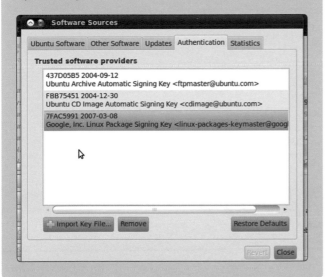

⚠ Software with backports

On your Linux travels you may encounter the term 'backports'. Ultimately, this is a way to get software designed for newer versions of Ubuntu into your current installation. Normally, the Ubuntu developers will focus on packaging up new programs for the version of Ubuntu that's currently in development, leaving the existing release for security and bug fixes.

This keeps everything stable, but it does mean that sometimes the latest-and-greatest software isn't easily available. There's a way round this: some developers will bundle up software from a newer Ubuntu release, re-compile it for the older version, and make it available in a repository known as 'backports'. There are multiple backport repositories (aka repos), so Google up the term and you'll find plenty of interesting sources of software.

5 Add the .deb location

There's one more thing we need to do, though: we need to tell Synaptic exactly where it can get packages from. We need to look for a repository address that starts with 'deb'. On the Google site we see that it's:

deb http://dl.google.com/linux/deb/ stable non-free main

We copy this entire line to the clipboard and go back into Synaptic. Now we click on the Other Software tab and the Add button (bottom-left), before pasting the repository information into the box (right-click in the box or use Ctrl+v to paste):

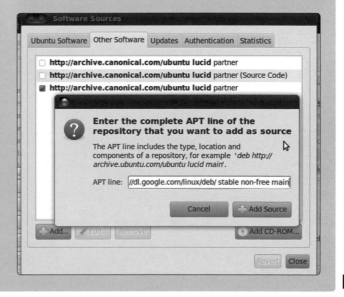

⚠ Cleaning up old packages

One final note on advanced package management: outside of Synaptic there's another tool that you'll find useful. Click System > Administration > Computer Janitor from the main desktop menu to start this small utility:

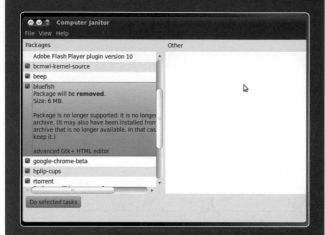

It's a rather basic-looking tool, but it helps you to identify wastage on the system. For instance, if you install program A it might install dependencies B and C. If you then remove program A, you'll still have dependencies B and C on the system, even though they're not being used. The Janitor will alert you to this fact and give you the option of removing packages that are no longer needed.

We recommend running it every now and then, especially after any major package work – such as uninstalling lots of programs – so that you can ensure that there's nothing pointless loitering on your drive.

6 Locate the new software

After clicking Add Source, we see the Google repository in the list. Finally, we need to tell Synaptic to scan for newly available packages, so we close the Software Sources dialog box to return back to the main Synaptic window, and then click the Reload button in the top-left of the screen:

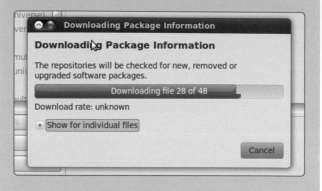

7 And install it!

A flurry of progress bars whizz by as the various repositories are checked; this can take a few minutes. When it's finished, we type 'chrome' into the search box at the top of the Synaptic window and see the results: 'google-chrome-beta' is available for us to install:

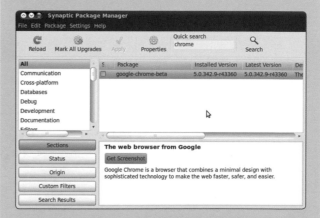

Now, you could ask why we've taken this approach when we could have directly downloaded a .deb file from Google's site and double-clicked it to install. Yes, that is an option. But that's only a one-off: by adding the repository, we now get updates to Google Chrome through Ubuntu's update manager, as it now scans Google's repositories as well as its own for updates. Additionally, if Google makes more software available through its repositories it'll be ready to go in one click from the package manager.

ADMINISTRATION
Linux security

If this were a Windows manual you'd be expecting a rather large section on security, but in the world of Linux there really are very few things to be concerned about. In Linux's history there have only been a handful of viruses, and most of those were proof-of-concept projects that didn't have a malicious payload. Equally, because software goes through the repository filtering system as described in the previous subsection, it's orders of magnitude safer than the typical Windows approach of finding a random Setup.exe file on the Internet and running it.

So, ultimately, you don't have to take an active security role in Linux – no virus checkers to buy, no malware finders to run in the background or anything like that. Nonetheless, keeping up to date with security updates (as covered in the next subsection) is a good idea, and there are a couple of things you can do to give yourself extra peace of mind.

Choosing a strong password

First up is a good password. The most rock-solid operating system in the world can be broken down if your password is your spouse or pet's name. By default Linux doesn't let anyone connect to your machine from the outside world, but if your computer is accessible by others, perhaps people you don't trust 100%, it's a good idea to create a strong password. You can do this in the user management tool described earlier, or (more simply) go to System > Preferences > About Me on the desktop menu:

Running the user information tool.

www.passwordmeter.com is a site that can rate the strength of a password.

Click Change Password in the top-right; you'll first be prompted for your current password, to prove that you have the right to change it, before entering the new one.

It is absolutely a good idea to use passwords that don't match any word in the English language. Particularly ambitious crackers can use 'dictionary attacks' which try to guess your password by bombarding login screens with combinations of words. Of course, unless someone is sat directly at your machine and you're the sole owner of doomsday device activation codes, it's unlikely that anyone would go to that extent to break your security, but it's still good practice.

Some administrators advocate using totally gibberish-looking passwords like 'fQn5d26toJ2id'. However, there's nothing at all memorable here: unless you've got a superbrain you'll need to have it written down for a while until it works with muscle memory guiding your fingers. And if it's written down, it's not secure. So we recommend finding two distinct words, such as 'jelly' and 'buddhism', and sewing them together with some numbers. You can use '1' to replace 'i', and '3' to replace 'E' for instance: 'j3llybuddh1sm'. That's actually memorable, yet sufficiently silly and unlikely that your account won't be broken in a hurry.

It's also a good idea to have different passwords for different logins. Admittedly, life would be a lot easier with a single password for everything, but that really is putting all of your eggs into one basket. If someone gets your login password, they could then get access to your email, Facebook, and – worst of all – your PayPal account!

Setting up a firewall

Let's move on to the second area of consideration in Linux security: firewalls. In its default installation, Ubuntu doesn't need a firewall, and you won't find any such utilities in the software menu. There are no open network ports in a stock Ubuntu installation so there's no way that a remote machine on the big, bad Internet can connect to yours and start poking around.

However, if you start running some server software, such as the Apache web server and BitTorrent server described in Section 7 (Advanced Linux), you may need a firewall. For instance, if you have a local network of machines and you don't want Apache to be accessible from outside of the network (ie on the wider Internet), you'll need to install a firewall on the machine that's running Apache.

1 Install Firestarter

Click Applications > Ubuntu Software Centre, then search for 'Firestarter' and install it:

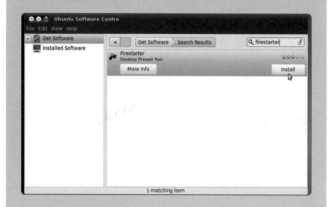

2 Start it up

Technically, Linux does include a firewall subsystem but Ubuntu doesn't include a graphical tool to manipulate it. Firestarter provides exactly what we need, though, and after installation you'll find it in System > Administration > Firestarter. A wizard will appear:

3 Choose the network device

In the next screen you'll be asked to select the network device that is connected to the Internet:

This is usually eth0 for a wired network and eth1 for wireless. If your Internet modem or router gives you an IP address automatically (the majority of setups) then check the 'IP address is assigned via DHCP' box and click Forward.

4 Enable connection sharing

On the next screen you can enable Internet connection sharing:

If you want others on your local network to connect to the Internet via you, instead of via the router/modem directly, check the box here. (If you want to choose 'enable DHCP' as well you'll need to install the dhcp3-server package and restart the wizard.) Click Forward and then Save at the final screen to store your settings.

5 The main screen

Then you'll see the main network activity screen:

Currently, all network ports are blocked – nobody can access them from the outside world. For instance, if you're running the Apache web server then nobody else will be able to connect to port 80 on your machine.

⚠ Firestarter options

Firestarter is an extremely capable tool: you can set up rules for outgoing ports as well as ingoing ports, view blocked connection attempts and even prioritise network activity for certain types of usage scenario (eg desktops vs servers). See Edit > Preferences and Help > Online User's Manual (have Firefox running first) for much more information on this powerful little app.

Firestarter is packed with advanced settings to tweak.

6 Open a new port

To rectify this, click the Policy tab and then right-click under the 'Allow service' column and choose 'Add Rule':

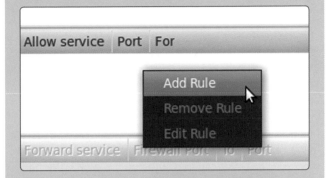

Now you can enter the port number that you wish to open (or choose 'HTTP' from the Name list and you'll see that it selects port 80 automatically). You can choose whether to allow access to anyone, those on the LAN (local area network, if applicable) or specific IP addresses or networks. You can provide a comment for your rule too:

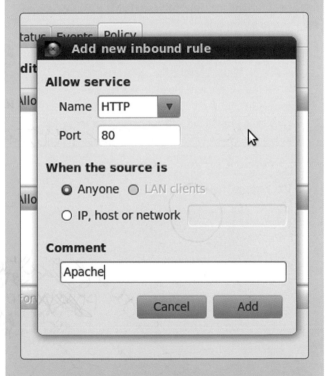

Now back in Firestarter's Policy view, you'll see the new rule: click the green tick icon in the top toolbar to activate your changes. Now other users on the local network or wide Internet should be able to access your Apache installation (depending on the option you chose).

ADMINISTRATION
Software updates

One of the great benefits about free and open-source software such as Linux is that anyone can peer under the hood. Any software developer can download the source code, the original human-readable recipe, that makes up Linux and look for ways to make the operating system even better. And if he or she discovers a weakness – such as a part of the code that could potentially become a security bug one day – then he or she can fix it and send the updated version to the maintainers.

Consequently, whenever any security issues are found in Linux then they're fixed extremely swiftly. This is in stark contrast to closed operating systems that could be chock-full of security holes waiting to be exploited – nobody except the original developers can look at the code. The open-source nature of Linux development means that potential problems can be caught early, while they're small, instead of turning into huge disasters that wreak havoc on the Internet for months.

1 Run the Update Manager
You may have already seen the Update Manager in Ubuntu if you're regularly connected to the Internet – it pops up periodically to let you know that new packages are available in the online Ubuntu repositories. If not, or you want to launch it manually, go to System > Administration > Update Manager in the desktop menu:

2 View the list of updates
The program will update its database of packages and then present you with a list of the new versions:

Viewing the list of available updates.

You can click on any of the entries in the list and then the 'Description of update' toggle box to view information on the fix(es) in the update:

Many of the descriptions are highly technical and geared towards developers, but they can give you an idea of what's going on. In the list you'll see the size of the packages: if you're on a limited connection – eg you're on dial-up and only want updates for certain key packages that you use – you can use the checkboxes next to the entries in the list to de-select packages. Note that some packages are dependencies of others, however, so you might not be able to de-select one without de-selecting another.

3 Install new packages

You can always refresh the view of the latest available updates with the Check button, and then click Install Updates to proceed:

Grabbing the new packages from the Internet.

Depending on how many updates are available and the speed of your connection, the process could take anywhere between a couple of minutes to a couple of hours. Still, while they're downloading there's nothing stopping you from doing your usual work (although most of your bandwidth will be taken up!).

The various types of updates

Although the Update Manager is designed to be a simple tool that keeps out of your way, there are a few options available to customise its behaviour. Click the Settings button in the bottom-left of the window to bring up this screen:

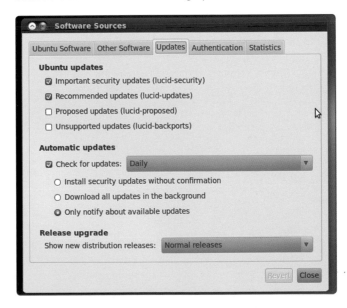

You might recognise the tabs at the top of the window – it's the same Software Sources window we were dealing with in the Synaptic subsection earlier. This time, though, we're in the Updates tab, and you can see what different types of updates are available. These are:

■ **Important security updates** – Vital packages that are part of the base system of Ubuntu, and maintained by the paid developers who work on the distribution. It's absolutely essential to have this checked.

■ **Recommended updates** – Not just for security, these are also fixes for small bugs and issues across the wider range of community-supported software in the vast Ubuntu repositories. We highly recommend keeping this option checked too.

■ **Proposed updates** – These are new packages pushed out by the developers for testing. They may contain security or bug fixes (or both), but they're intended for Ubuntu developers for testing before they're released out to every single user. A pre-testing update package could actually bring about other problems, so we recommend steering clear of this one.

■ **Unsupported updates** – These are usually major new versions of software created by the community. For instance, Ubuntu 10.04 is supplied with Firefox 3.6, and they will continue to support version 3.6 throughout the lifespan of this version of Ubuntu. So that the OS doesn't keep going through radical changes, the Ubuntu team applies fixes to existing versions, saving a huge wave of all-new software for the next big release of Ubuntu. However, if Firefox 4.0 comes out and you want to try it before the next Ubuntu release, someone in the community might 'backport' it to Ubuntu 10.04 and put it in this repository. Therefore this can be useful when you've been running Linux for a while, but it can break programs. If you want pure stability, leave it unchecked; if you fancy living life on the cutting edge, try this.

Then you can tell the Update Manager how often you want it to check for new packages. If you're on a slower connection and find that a daily check keeps interfering with your work, switch this to weekly or fortnightly. Alternatively, you can tell the program to not download anything in the background, and merely let you know in advance if new packages are available. Then you'll have to give it your express permission to start the package download job.

Notice the 'Release upgrade' drop-down menu at the bottom: this looks for major new versions of Ubuntu. There are two types of releases in the Ubuntu world: normal versions, which arrive every six months, and LTS (Long Term Support) versions, which arrive intermittently and receive updates for a much longer period. The version of Ubuntu on your disc, 10.04, is an LTS release and we recommend sticking with it. You can always update to a new release when it becomes available, but the Ubuntu team might make some changes that diverge from the guides in this book, so be aware!

07.
Advanced Linux

In this section

ADVANCED LINUX
The command line

Typing in words to make the computer do things – who wants to fiddle around with that? Can't we just do everything with the GUI? Well, yes, for day-to-day desktop usage you never need to touch the command line interface (CLI) in Linux. However, the CLI is exceptionally powerful and lets you accomplish certain tasks much faster than in the file manager.

Additionally, the CLI lets you explore deeper into the system and fix problems that may not be solvable via the regular graphical interface. For these reasons it's well worth learning how to harness the power of the command line – after reading this section you'll be empowered to manage your Linux installation like a full-time system administrator.

Now, if you've come from a DOS or Windows background you might not be relishing the idea of working with the command line. After all, the implementations in those systems are pretty bare-bones and fiddly to deal with (although recent versions of Windows are getting better). Linux is worlds apart, though: the CLI has many helpful features to save you time and make working at the prompt a much more pleasant experience.

Command line essentials

Let's get started. The program that provides access to the command line in Linux is called the terminal, so click Applications > Accessories > Terminal from the desktop menu to open one up. You'll see a new window appear on the screen that's mostly blank, except for some text in the top-left corner.

That text is called the prompt, and it contains some useful tidbits of information. In our example it says:

```
mike@mike-laptop:~$
```

The first bit, 'mike', is the login name of the current user, so that will be your login name. After the '@' symbol we have the hostname of the machine – that is, the name you provided when installing the system. Then there's a colon (:), followed by what looks like a squiggle (~). This shows the current directory (folder) that we're in – but we'll come to that in a moment. Then there's a dollar sign, which says: we're ready for input.

Trying a command

Let's enter a command. Type in 'ls' and press Enter. Most Linux commands have very short names; it might not be obvious at first what they do, but their terseness will save you a huge amount of time in the long run. Note that as with filenames, commands are case-sensitive. (You'll find a command reference in the Appendix for a quick reminder of the most useful commands.)

Here, 'ls' means 'list', and simply lists the files contained inside the current directory (like 'DIR' in DOS/Windows). When you open a terminal via the program menu, it will start off inside your home directory – that is, /home/username. In this case, 'ls' shows the files inside /home/mike.

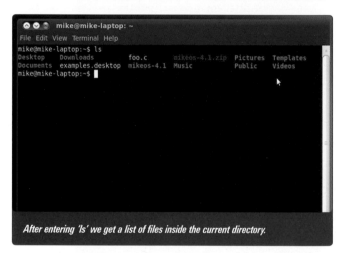

After entering 'ls' we get a list of files inside the current directory.

You'll notice that the output of 'ls' contains multiple colours. The most important colour is blue: anything that is blue is a directory (folder) that you can go into. You can quickly view the contents of a directory using 'ls' with the directory name – eg 'ls photos'. As you use the command line you'll discover other colours as well, such as red for compressed archives and purple for images.

Now, almost every command can take options or 'parameters': extra bits of information to modify the command. These are denoted by dash (-) characters. For instance, instead of entering just 'ls', try 'ls -l' (ls space dash l).

This '-l' option tells 'ls' to operate in long-listing mode, so it shows the files and directories in a single column with lots of information next to them. For instance:

```
drwxr-xr-x 3 mike mike 4096 2010-03-20 14:37 Desktop
```

A window, ready for your input.

Using 'ls -l' we get the long-listing form of the command.

You'll see files and directories called, for example, .pulse-cookie, .bashrc, .gnome2 and so forth. You don't need to know what these do; they're simply configuration settings for the various programs running on your machine. As you install and run new programs you'll see more hidden settings folders here.

Why are they normally hidden? Firstly, because they're settings files they should be kept out of the way – you don't want to accidentally delete files or make changes. Secondly, when you have lots of settings files and folders it can look very cluttered, so when you're working with your regular day-to-day files you don't want to be looking at config files all the time.

You'll also notice with 'ls -la' that there are two blue directory entries at the start of the listing: '.' and '..'. The single dot refers to the current directory, and the '..' refers to the directory below this one. But how do we move into another directory? The answer is the 'cd' command – 'change directory'.

The first two bits here are the permissions and links, but you don't need to be concerned with them now. With 'mike mike 4096' you see the user and group that owns the file, along with its size in bytes. After that is the date and time that the entry was modified, along with its name. (If you ever change the permissions of a directory in the future, note that directories have to be executable for them to be accessible by normal users.)

Changing the listing view

This listing mode is useful, but not perfect. All file sizes are listed in bytes, so if you have a file that's, say, 229768415 bytes, you have to make mental calculations to work out what that is in normal sizes (kilobytes or megabytes). Fortunately there's an answer: the '-h' option, which means 'human readable'. You can tack it on to the end of the 'ls' command with 'ls -l -h'.

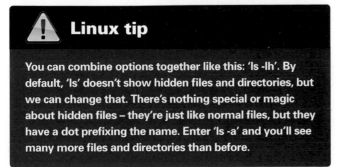

With the '-h' option we get human readable file sizes.

⚠ Linux tip

You can combine options together like this: 'ls -lh'. By default, 'ls' doesn't show hidden files and directories, but we can change that. There's nothing special or magic about hidden files – they're just like normal files, but they have a dot prefixing the name. Enter 'ls -a' and you'll see many more files and directories than before.

Switching to a different directory

Enter 'cd Desktop', for instance, and you'll switch into the Desktop directory (ie the folder which contains files shown on your desktop), and your prompt will be updated to show this. Enter 'ls' to see the files contained therein.

Switch to another directory with 'cd directoryname' and then enter 'ls' to view the contents.

To go back to the directory you were in before – that is, the directory below the current one – enter 'cd ..' (cd space dot dot). At any point you can enter 'cd' on its own to return to your home directory. Keep an eye on your prompt as a reminder of where you are: as you may have discovered, the aforementioned squiggle (~) tilde character refers to your home directory.

You can use the full locations (aka paths) of files and directories with commands, separating the directories with forward slashes: eg 'cd /home/mike/Music' or 'ls -l /home/dave/README.TXT'. If you want to find out where on the system a file or directory lives, use 'locate': eg 'locate README'.

ADVANCED LINUX
File operations

So, we know how to move around inside our directories and see what files are contained therein – we know how to navigate around the system. Now let's look at some file operations. Anything you can do in the file manager, you can do at the command line, although the reverse isn't always true, as we'll see! Let's start by copying a file, using the 'cp' command:

```
cp file1 file2
```

Copying a file with 'cp' is easy: just provide the name of the file you want to copy, and the new filename.

This copies file1 (which must already exist) to a new file called file2. If you want to copy multiple files, you need to provide the name of a directory into which you want to copy them:

```
cp file1 file2 myfolder
```

With multiple files, you specify a directory into which you want to copy them.

Remember that directories are separated by slashes, and can be denoted with slashes at the end, so the above command could also be written as:

```
cp file1 file2 myfolder/
```

To copy a directory we need to use an option called '-r', which means 'recursive': eg 'cp -r old-dir new-dir'. This 'recurses' into the directory and copies all files and sub-directories inside it too.

Moving and renaming files

What about if you want to move a file to another location? The answer is another two-letter command: 'mv'. For example:

```
mv bunny.jpg mypics
```

This moves bunny.jpg into the mypics folder. Note that 'mv' will move to another filename if you don't specify an existing directory – it renames the file. So 'mv bunny.jpg cutebunny.jpg' just changes its name.

Earlier we mentioned that '..' is the directory beneath the current one. So, if you're inside /home/mike/mypics and you have a file called hamster.jpg, you can move it down into your home directory like this:

```
mv hamster.jpg ..
```

In this screenshot we're going into a directory called 'tmp' and moving 'rabbit.jpg' into the directory below it – the directory we were just in.

To delete a file we use the 'rm' command – 'remove'. Be careful with this, as there's no recycle bin/trash can or any other way to recover a file when it has been deleted using the command line. Example:

```
rm filename
```

Delete files using the 'rm' command.

You can delete multiple files ('rm file1 file2 file3'), but if you want to delete a directory, you have to give 'rm' the '-r' option for 'recursive' – ie go inside it and delete any files first:

```
rm -r photos_folder
```

If you want to create a new directory, use 'mkdir' (make directory) like this: 'mkdir mypics'. To see how much space a directory occupies on the disk, use 'du -h directory'.

Master the power of wildcards

So far so good, but these facilities are easily available in your file manager. Where the command line really shines is with something called wildcards. A wildcard is a special symbol that can be replaced by anything else – any other character or characters that can be part of a filename. The most useful one is *, the asterisk character available via Shift+8 on most keyboards. This wildcard character means: any combination of letters and numbers.

Consider this example. Say you have a folder full of images. Some end in .png, some in .gif, and some in .jpg. If you enter 'ls' on its own, it will show all the files. But if you enter this command:

```
ls *.jpg
```

it will only display files that end with .jpg. The asterisk wildcard expands to match any combination of letters and numbers before .jpg. Try it with some other file endings. You can include asterisks anywhere, and have multiple wildcards:

```
ls *cat*
```

Here, in the second 'ls' command, we're using wildcards to only show files that have a capital A in the filename.

This will show all files that have 'cat' in the filename (remember that filenames are case-sensitive). So this would show mycat.jpg, cat.gif and supermegacat.

Another wildcard is '?', the question mark. This just stands for a single number or letter, as opposed to any amount of numbers or letters with the asterisk. For example, 'ls ?cat.jpg' will show 'acat.jpg' but not 'mycat.jpg'.

Using wildcards you can perform operations at the command line that would take hours of painstaking labour in a file manager. For instance, imagine you have a large, unsorted collection of hundreds of photos in a directory like this:

```
photocat0001.png
dansdog.jpg
aquarium_27.jpg
090910_tiddles.png
bestdogphoto.jpg
largedog2pic08.jpg
12_mice_large.png
...
```

You want to move all the ones with 'dog' in the filename to the 'my_photos' directory – but only the files that end in .jpg. If you were to do this in your file manager, it would take hours: you might be able to tell your file manager to select only files with 'dog' in them, but then you'd still have to go through and pick out the ones with .jpg, then hold the right combination of Shift/Alt/Ctrl+click to select them, and hope it all works correctly.

No thanks. It's extremely simple at the command line with the knowledge you've gleaned:

```
mv *dog*.jpg my_photos
```

There we go. A job that could have taken hours, executed in one step. Of course, this is just a specific example, but you will find many situations in which wildcards are tremendously useful and will save you massive amounts of time.

ADVANCED LINUX
Useful utilities

A t this point you can freely move around the filesystem and manipulate files. Here we'll move on to some of the most useful tools you can use at the command line to inspect files and get more information about them.

If you come across a filename with no extension (or an extension you don't recognise), try running 'file' with its filename. For instance, enter 'cd /usr/share/example-content' to go to Ubuntu's folder of sample files, and enter 'ls' to see what's in there. Then run 'file Derivatives_of_Ubuntu.doc'. You'll see lots of information on the .doc file as shown in the screenshot – all without having to open it up in a word processor. Try it for images and other files.

The 'file' command is mighty useful for quickly determining file information.

At this point you might be getting a bit tired of typing in the full filenames each time, so here's a short cut: tab completion. Instead of typing 'file Derivatives_of_Ubuntu.doc', just type 'file D' and then press the tab key. Voila: the full filename is automatically filled out for you. This is a wonderful time-saver for long file and directory names, and you'll find yourself hovering one finger over the tab key as you do more work at the CLI. If you try to tab-complete a filename where there are multiple possibilities for completion, the CLI will show you what's available, so enter another few letters to narrow it down and press tab again.

Retrieve previous commands

Another vital short cut is command history. Using the up and down cursor keys you can cycle through the commands you've typed in previously – then use the left and right cursor keys to edit the command (if required) and Enter to run it again. Enter 'history' on its own to see a list of your most recent commands.

Enter 'history' to view previous commands.

At the command line, you can run any program available in your menus. For instance, if you have an HTML file and want to view it in Firefox, enter 'firefox filename.html'. To open a file in a text editor, enter 'gedit filename.txt'. However, there's a quick way to view a text file that doesn't involve firing up the whole graphical editor: using 'cat'. This 'concatenates' a file to the screen, so try it with a text file: 'cat README.TXT', for instance.

What if the file is too big, and just scrolls off the screen? There's another program you can use: 'less'. This is a scrolling text-file viewer that lets you pan up and down in a file. Find a text file and try it with 'less filename.txt'. Use the up and down cursor keys to scroll through the

Use the 'less' tool to view text files.

document, and press Q to quit. To search for a word, press the forward slash (/) key and type the word you're looking for.

If you want to get help on a command or program, use the 'man' utility – short for 'manual page viewer'. For instance, enter 'man ls' and you'll get the guide for the 'ls' command and all of its available options – it's very dull, dry information, but nonetheless useful as a reference. Use the same keys as with 'less' to scroll, search and quit.

Almost every command has a manual page: use 'man' to read it (eg 'man ls').

Redirecting output to a file

Sometimes you might enter a command that produces a lot of output – too much to fit on the screen. Or perhaps you want to save the output of a command without having to copy and paste every screen of text into a file. Thankfully, there's an easy way to sort out these problems: command redirection. Using the greater-than (>) symbol you can send, or redirect, the output of a command to a file:

```
ls > listing.txt
```

Here we're redirecting the output of 'ls' to a file called 'list', and then using 'cat' to show the contents of that file.

You can then open listing.txt in your text editor or view it with 'less'. A single greater-than sign creates a new file or totally overwrites the contents of an existing file; if you want to append the output on to an existing file, use two greater-than signs together:

```
ls >> listing.txt
```

We're appending the output of 'ls' on to the file 'list', so that it now contains two listings.

Another technique, similar to redirecting, is piping. This is the process of directly sending the output of a command straight to another program. For instance, say we want to view the output of the 'ls' command in the 'less' viewer, without having to redirect it into a text file first. We use the pipe symbol (|, usually shared with the backslash key on your keyboard) like this:

```
ls | less
```

Using the pipe character we can send output from a command straight to the 'less' viewer.

Working with compressed archives

Lastly, let's have a quick look at archives. You will often come across files ending in .tar.gz or .tar.bz2, which are compressed archives used to distribute programs and other files across the Internet. You can extract these in the file manager, but if you need to do it at the command line, here's how it works. For both .tar.gz and .tar.bz2 files:

```
tar xfv filename
```

Usually this will create a new directory containing the uncompressed files, as you'll see on the screen. Linux can easily handle .zip files too:

```
unzip filename
```

What if we want to create an archive? We can use .tar.gz, which is a fast compression method that's supported by most operating systems. The command takes a directory name as follows:

```
tar cfvz filename.tar.gz directory
```

This creates a new archive called filename.tar.gz using the contents of 'directory'. Alternatively, we can use the .tar.bz2 format, which generates smaller files but requires more time to compress and expand:

```
tar cfvj filename.tar.bz2 directory
```

For .zip files, which is the best format if you're planning to share files with Windows users, you can create archives from directories like this:

```
zip -ry filename.zip directory
```

Extracting files at the command line is easy.

Finishing off

By now you should feel very comfortable with the command line: you can navigate around your computer, run important commands and manage the output. You can string commands together, determine types of files and extract archives. With wildcards you can perform operations that would take forever in a file manager. You've got the tools to really master Linux.

In the Appendix you'll find a list of the most commonly used commands, so give it a read through and keep it nearby for future reference. We'll finish off this section with a few handy keyboard combinations that are worth remembering:

- Ctrl+l – clear the screen.
- Ctrl+c – kill the currently running program straight away (eg a good way to interrupt very long file listing processes).
- Ctrl+z – put the currently running program into the background (resume it with 'fg').
- Ctrl+d – exit the terminal session (shorter than typing 'exit').

Want to stop a long command from running? Just hit Ctrl+c.

.tar.bz2 is a powerful compression format but needs more time than .tar.gz and .zip to compress and decompress.

ADVANCED LINUX
Enabling remote logins

If your PC is connected to a network, you can install a piece of software that lets you connect to your machine from anywhere else on the network and run commands, just as if you were sitting in front of it. There are two reasons why you may want to do this:

1 To control a machine remotely for convenience. Say your main Linux machine is in the upstairs of your house, and you're sitting in the garden with a laptop. If you need to perform a command on the Linux box – say, making a file available on your web server (which we'll cover later in this section) – you'd normally have to put down your drink and trudge into the house. With remote logins, you can quickly access your machine and run the command you want without so much as standing up. You can even connect to your Linux PC over the Internet if required.

2 Fixing problems. Linux is extremely reliable, but if you've got a problem with semi-broken hardware it's possible it could lock up your display and keyboard. With remote logins enabled, you can log into the machine from another and shut it down gracefully.

The program we're going to use is called SSH: the Secure Shell. This encrypts connections between your Linux box and anything that connects to it, so if you're connecting via the Internet then nobody will be able to snoop at your commands. The command to access an SSH connection on a remote machine ('ssh') is included as standard on Linux and Mac OS X; on Windows you'll need a free program like PuTTY (www.chiark.greenend.org.uk/~sgtatham/putty/) in order to access your Linux box from afar.

1 Install the SSH server

On your Linux machine, the first thing we need to do is install the SSH server: SSHD. Open a terminal and enter this command:

```
sudo apt-get install openssh-server
```

This will retrieve the server from the Ubuntu package repositories on the Internet, and start it running.

2 Finding your IP address

Now you can connect to your Linux box from anywhere on your local network. However, you first need to find out the IP address (the number that shows where it is on the network). Enter this command:

```
ifconfig | grep 'inet addr'
```

That's a pipe character between ifconfig and grep. You will see output similar to this screenshot:

Normally, entering 'ifconfig' on its own spews out a huge amount of information, so in this case we pipe the output to a text-filtering command, 'grep', which then just shows the lines containing 'inet addr'.

Among this information you'll see IP addresses after the 'inet addr:' parts. You can ignore the one that says '127.0.0.1' as that simply points to the local machine – it's a special address that always points to the PC you're using. So we want the first one – 10.0.2.19. This is the IP address of our Linux box on the network, and the address we can use to access it.

3 Connect to your box (local network)

Now, go to another machine on your network. If it's another Linux PC or a Mac running Mac OS X, open a terminal and enter:

```
ssh username@IP address
```

Replace 'username' with the user you want to log in as, and IP address with the full IP address of the remote machine. In our case, we want to log in as 'mike' on the PC that has the address 10.0.2.19, so we use:

```
ssh mike@10.0.2.19
```

After a few moments you'll be prompted for your password, and you'll be logged in.

It works! Here we've logged in to our Linux machine from a Mac that's on the same network.

You can now use the command line as described in the previous section, just as if you were sitting at the machine. When you're done, type 'exit' to quit the session or press Ctrl+d. (Tip: If you're trying to fix a problematic remote machine and need to shut it down, enter 'sudo halt'.)

4 Connect from the Internet

If your Linux machine is connected to the Internet and you want to be able to access it from another machine on the Internet, you'll need to do two things. First, instead of using the IP address discovered with the 'ifconfig' command, which only applies to the local network, you'll need to find out the IP address given by your Internet service provider for the whole Internet. You can do this at www.whatsmyip.org (or use Google to find 'what is my IP' for similar sites).

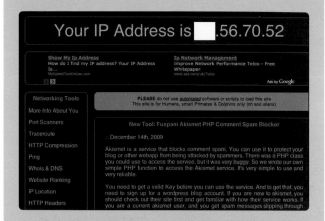

Next, you'll need to make sure that the SSH port is accessible through your Internet router or modem. By default SSH connections are made through network port 22, so consult your router or modem's documentation to find out how to make that port open. (If you have multiple machines connected to a router, make sure the router is forwarding port 22 to your Linux box.) Once this is done, you will be able to log in over the Internet using 'ssh username@IP address' as described before.

Transferring files

Handily, you can transfer files using SSH too. The command you need is 'scp', and it copies a file over a SSH connection to the machine running the SSH server. So, on a remote machine you can copy a file to your Linux PC like this:

```
scp filename user@IP address:/path/you/want
```

A colon separates the IP address and the location you want to store the file (usually the user's home directory, as you won't be able to write files in most other places). Back to our example, on our Mac (on the local network) we copy a file like this:

```
scp photo.jpg mike@10.0.2.19:/home/mike
```

You can copy multiple files by specifying them before the user@ part, or even use wildcards to copy a large number

of files: 'scp *.jpg ...' to copy all JPG images.

The SSH server configuration file is /etc/ssh/sshd_config, and lets you change the port number that SSH operates on among other things. Enter 'man sshd_config' for more information on that file, and 'man ssh' for general SSH options. If you make any changes to the configuration file, you'll need to restart the SSH server with 'sudo /etc/init.d/ssh restart'. And if you ever want to remove the SSH server, run 'sudo apt-get autoremove openssh-server'.

PuTTY is an excellent free SSH connection program for connecting to your Linux box from Windows.

ADVANCED LINUX
Editing and saving

With command line knowledge safely stored in your brain, you can explore the system and view configuration files. Most critical system config files are stored in the /etc directory, so you can see what's available by entering 'cd /etc' and then 'ls'. There are a lot of files in there and the exact workings of them is way beyond the scope of this book – but unless you have a major problem with your installation you won't need to change them.

Nonetheless, for future reference it's good to know what some of them do, so we'll list the most important ones here. If you have a problem with Linux and post a message on a website forum, you may be given instructions to view or modify one of these files. Note that almost every file outside of your home directory can only be modified by the root (administrator) user, so you can't just edit them with 'gedit filename'. Instead, you need to run 'sudo' (which means 'do the command as the superuser', aka root) like this:

```
sudo gedit filename
```

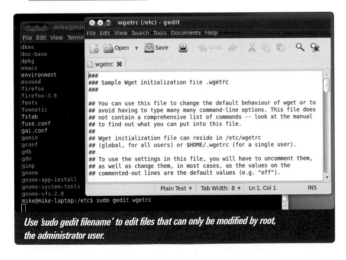

Use 'sudo gedit filename' to edit files that can only be modified by root, the administrator user.

You will be prompted for your password. (Tip: you can start a whole root terminal session with 'sudo bash' – but be extremely careful, as one wrongly typed command could totally wipe out your installation!)

Here are the most important files and directories to be aware of and what they do:

■ **/etc/lsb-release** – Contains information describing the distribution and exact version of Linux that you're running.

■ **/etc/hostname** – The name associated with this particular machine, used to identify it on the network. You'll see this name in the command line prompt – eg 'bob-desktop'.

■ **/etc/init.d** – A directory containing system startup scripts. These enable hardware, mount drives, configure networking and so forth. Because system updates can overwrite these files, it's a good idea to leave them alone and add anything you want to start in /etc/rc.local.

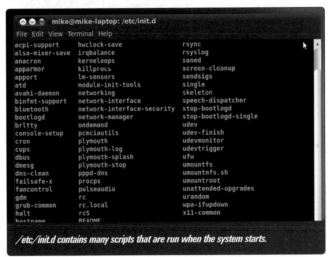

/etc/init.d contains many scripts that are run when the system starts.

■ **/etc/rc.local** – A modifiable system startup script. If you need to run a (non-graphical) command during the boot process, put the command before the 'exit 0' line here. Add an ampersand (&) after the command if you want it to run in the background and not hold up the boot process.

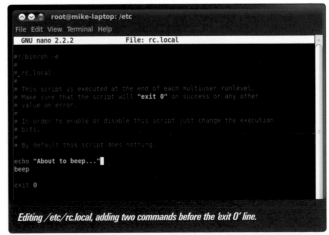

Editing /etc/rc.local, adding two commands before the 'exit 0' line.

■ **/etc/default/** – This directory contains default settings for various system programs and features. For instance, default settings for power management are stored here in the file 'acpi-support', and the scripts for power management are in /etc/acpi.

■ **/etc/bash.bashrc** – The configuration file for the shell (command line). It's a well-commented file with lots of information on how to change the prompt, tweak features etc. Note that this applies to all users on the system: for user-specific changes, edit .bashrc in the user's home directory.

```
root@mike-laptop: /etc
File Edit View Terminal Help
# System-wide .bashrc file for interactive bash(1) shells.

# To enable the settings / commands in this file for login shells as well,
# this file has to be sourced in /etc/profile.

# If not running interactively, don't do anything
[ -z "$PS1" ] && return

# check the window size after each command and, if necessary,
# update the values of LINES and COLUMNS.
shopt -s checkwinsize

# set variable identifying the chroot you work in (used in the prompt below)
if [ -z "$debian_chroot" ] && [ -r /etc/debian_chroot ]; then
    debian_chroot=$(cat /etc/debian_chroot)
fi

# set a fancy prompt (non-color, overwrite the one in /etc/profile)
PS1='${debian_chroot:+($debian_chroot)}\u@\h:\w\$ '

# Commented out, don't overwrite xterm -T "title" -n "icontitle" by default.
# If this is an xterm set the title to user@host:dir
#case "$TERM" in
/etc/bash.bashrc
```

/etc/bash.bashrc is the place for system-wide customisations of the command line interface (aka shell).

■ **/etc/passwd and /etc/shadow** – Files that describe login accounts and passwords. Note that you can change a password using the 'passwd' command.

■ **/etc/sysctl.conf** – Settings and options for kernel features. Very advanced networking tutorials often describe changes you can make to this file.

■ **/etc/cron.daily/, /etc/cron.weekly/, /etc/cron.monthly/** – Inside these directories you'll find scripts that are executed every day, once a week and once a month respectively. These are normally system maintenance scripts, such as clearing up temporary files and compressing old logs. The program that executes these scripts is called 'cron' and its configuration file is /etc/crontab.

A look inside /etc/cron.daily and /etc/cron.weekly, showing the scripts that are to be run on a regular basis.

■ **/boot/grub/grub.cfg** – Settings for the GRUB boot loader. When your PC boots, your PC's BIOS loads the GRUB boot loader, which in turn loads the Linux kernel and starts the booting process. This file tells GRUB where to find the kernel, and how to boot any other operating systems that may be installed on the drive (eg Windows).

```
root@mike-laptop: ~
File Edit View Terminal Help
### BEGIN /etc/grub.d/10_linux ###
menuentry "Ubuntu, with Linux 2.6.32-16-generic" --class ubuntu --class gnu-linu
x --class gnu --class os {
        recordfail
        insmod ext2
        set root='(hd0,2)'
        search --no-floppy --fs-uuid --set d01787a2-ad1b-47bf-8c2e-2e81c3dcdff4
        linux   /boot/vmlinuz-2.6.32-16-generic root=UUID=d01787a2-ad1b-47bf-8c2
e-2e81c3dcdff4 ro   quiet splash
        initrd  /boot/initrd.img-2.6.32-16-generic
}
menuentry "Ubuntu, with Linux 2.6.32-16-generic (recovery mode)" --class ubuntu
--class gnu-linux --class gnu --class os {
        recordfail
        insmod ext2
        set root='(hd0,2)'
        search --no-floppy --fs-uuid --set d01787a2-ad1b-47bf-8c2e-2e81c3dcdff4
        echo    Loading Linux 2.6.32-16-generic ...
        linux   /boot/vmlinuz-2.6.32-16-generic root=UUID=d01787a2-ad1b-47bf-8c2
e-2e81c3dcdff4 ro single
        echo    Loading initial ramdisk ...
        initrd  /boot/initrd.img-2.6.32-16-generic
}
:
```

In /boot/grub/grub.cfg you'll find settings for loading the Linux kernel, as shown here.

■ **/var/log/auth.log** – This file lists all instances of users logging in and out (authenticating). As files in /var/log grow in size, periodically the system renames and compresses them, putting a new, empty file in place to save size. So auth.log has the most recent authentication entries, and auth.log.1 (or auth.log.1.gz) has older entries.

■ **/var/log/syslog** – A complete log of all system activity. This file can be very large, but you can view the most recent lines using the 'tail' command: eg 'tail -n30 /var/log/syslog' shows the 30 most recent lines in the system log. Older logs may be in syslog.1 as per the information in auth.log.

```
root@mike-laptop: ~
File Edit View Terminal Help
Mar 22 14:39:16 mike-laptop NetworkManager: <info>  (eth1): supplicant connectio
n state: disconnected -> scanning
Mar 22 14:39:17 mike-laptop anacron[5757]: Anacron 2.3 started on 2010-03-22
Mar 22 14:39:17 mike-laptop anacron[5757]: Normal exit (0 jobs run)
Mar 22 14:39:17 mike-laptop avahi-daemon[706]: Registering new address record fo
r fe80::221:ff:fe91:2917 on eth1.*.
Mar 22 14:39:26 mike-laptop kernel: [ 9559.797046] eth1: no IPv6 routers present
Mar 22 14:39:27 mike-laptop wpa_supplicant[734]: Trying to associate with 00:17:
f2:53:21:0c (SSID='MikeNet' freq=2422 MHz)
Mar 22 14:39:27 mike-laptop NetworkManager: <info>  (eth1): supplicant connectio
n state:  scanning -> associating
Mar 22 14:39:27 mike-laptop wpa_supplicant[734]: Association request to the driv
er failed
Mar 22 14:39:28 mike-laptop wpa_supplicant[734]: Associated with 00:17:f2:53:21:
0c
Mar 22 14:39:28 mike-laptop wpa_supplicant[734]: CTRL-EVENT-CONNECTED - Connecti
on to 00:17:f2:53:21:0c completed (auth) [id=0 id_str=]
Mar 22 14:39:28 mike-laptop NetworkManager: <info>  (eth1): supplicant connectio
n state:  associating -> associated
Mar 22 14:39:28 mike-laptop NetworkManager: <info>  (eth1): supplicant connectio
n state:  associated -> completed
Mar 22 14:39:28 mike-laptop NetworkManager: <info>  Activation (eth1/wireless) S
tage 2 of 5 (Device Configure) successful.  Connected to wireless network 'MikeN
et'.
```

/var/log/syslog is regularly updated behind the scenes: here it is showing status messages for wireless networking.

■ **/var/log/Xorg.0.log** – This is the log file for the X Window System, the base graphical layer (see the glossary in the appendix). If for some reason your desktop isn't loading normally and you're left at a purely text-mode command prompt, or something appears to be wrong with your display, look in here for any errors or warnings.

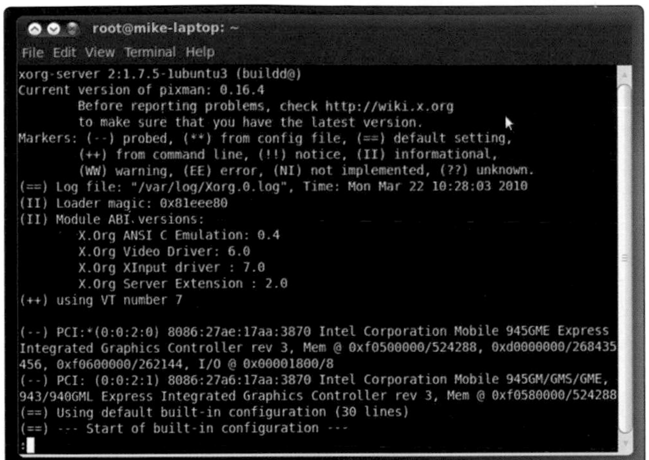

/var/log/Xorg.0.log shows X server activity, here detecting an on-board Intel graphics chip.

■ **/proc/mounts** – A non-editable file that shows which real and virtual devices are accessible on the system. If you plug in, for example, a USB key, information about it will appear here.

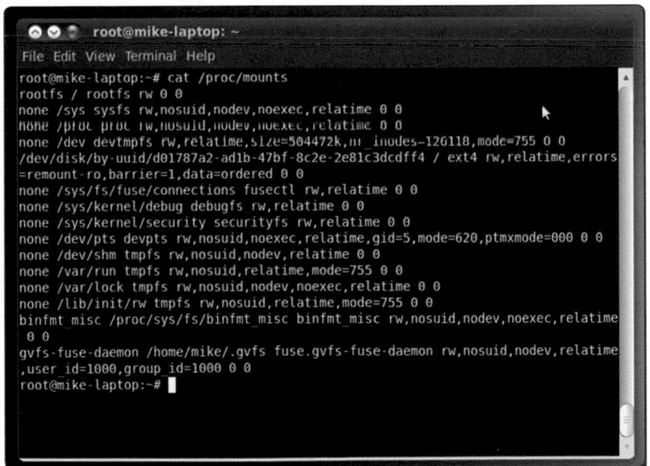

An example /proc/mounts: the entry that starts with /dev/disk is the main hard drive.

■ **/proc/modules** – This file shows the modules that are currently loaded into the kernel. Most modules are drivers for specific pieces of hardware, but some software features (eg relating to networking) can be loaded as modules too. You can find the modules in /lib/modules – there's a directory for your kernel version number.

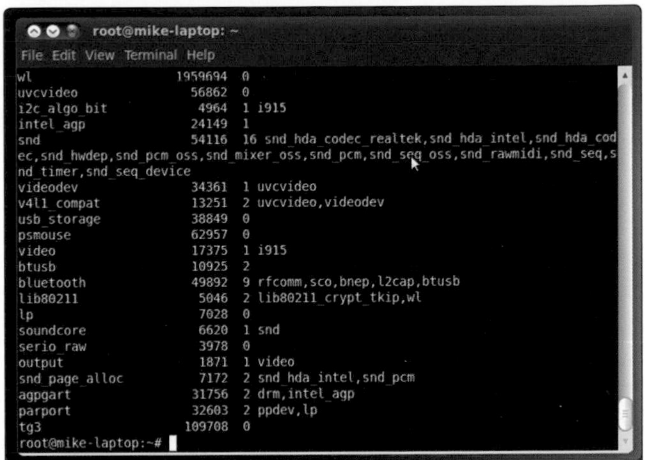

You can get information on loaded modules via /proc/modules, or enter 'lsmod' for a slightly more neatly formatted version.

If you're going to make some big changes to your system, it's a good idea to back up these files into your home directory so that you can restore them if something breaks later. Open a terminal and create a directory in which you're going to place the backups: eg 'mkdir system_files'. Then you can copy files into it – remember that many files are only readable as the root (administrator) user, so we need to precede the commands with 'sudo':

```
sudo cp /etc/rc.local system_files
```

That copies the /etc/rc.local file into your new system_files directory. As you'll recall from the command line guide earlier, when copying directories you need to specify the '-r' option:

```
sudo cp -r /etc/default system_files
```

To copy a file or directory back, you just reverse the process, eg:

```
sudo cp system_files/rc.local /etc
```

Or for a directory:

```
sudo cp -r system_files/default /etc
```

Note that you can add '-i' to a command to make it prompt you if it's going to do something potentially damaging, such as overwriting another file. This enables interrogative mode, so it's worth dropping in when you're about to do something major on the system and want to make sure you're not going to erase existing files. You can hit 'y' at the prompt(s) to confirm that you want to go ahead with the file copy operation.

ADVANCED LINUX
Your own web server

Underneath the modern, attractive desktop skin of Linux beats the heart of a high-performance, ultra-reliable server platform. Indeed, before Linux really started to make an impact in the desktop computing world it was in widespread use as a server – especially in the web server world. As large-scale consumer usage of the Internet took off in the late 1990s, more and more companies wanted a web presence, but without paying huge licensing fees for Unix, the traditional web server platform. Thanks to Linux being totally free, it rapidly shot to fame.

The web server software most commonly run on Linux is called Apache. This is the most popular web server in the world, with over 100 million websites and 54% market share. Yet while Apache is an astoundingly serious piece of software on large-scale servers, it's also perfectly

suited for running on home machines to share files around your network, or set up a personal website (if you have a permanently-on Internet connection). Here we're going to install Apache and show what you can do with it.

Even if you don't plan to run a website permanently from your home computer, the skills you'll learn here will come in very useful if you decided to set up a dedicated server later, whether it's in your office or on a remote machine at a hosting company. Alternatively, you may want to convert a computer from running another program to Apache.

Along with Linux and other Unix-like operating systems, Apache runs on Microsoft Windows, so if you want to improve the security in your company, but they won't budge from Windows on their servers, at least you can use your Apache skills to make things better.

1 Fetch the packages

First, open a terminal and enter this command to fetch the Apache packages from Ubuntu's servers and install it:

```
sudo apt-get install apache2
```

You may be prompted to hit the 'y' key to confirm installation. After the server is installed it will be started up automatically, as you'll see in the last lines of the output. For future reference you can stop Apache with 'sudo /etc/init.d/apache2 stop' and start it again with 'sudo /etc/init.d/apache2 start'.

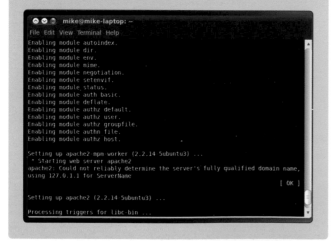

2 View the test page

With Apache running, open the Firefox web browser and type this into the address bar:

```
http://127.0.0.1
```

This is the special IP address of your local machine. It's a reserved address – whatever Linux machine you're on, it always points to the local system. You will see this cheerful congratulatory screen.

Here we can see that Apache is working properly and serving us an example page. Your website is ready to be constructed.

3 Edit the files

By default, Apache stores all of the files that it serves in the /var/www directory. If you go into there you'll see one file: index.html – that's the example file we're seeing. You can now copy other files into /var/www and edit index.html to your liking, but remember that because it's outside of your home directory, it won't be modifiable using your normal user account. So you'll need to use 'sudo cp' to copy files and 'sudo gedit index.html' to edit the main page.

Building your website

If you've never made a website before, there are plenty of resources available to give you the skills you need, such as Haynes' *Build Your Own Website* (ISBN 978-1-8442-5658-7). On the software side, you'll find some excellent free web editors available in the Ubuntu Software Centre – try Bluefish, Kompozer and Seamonkey Composer.

If you plan to use Apache to share files, you won't want to go about creating HTML files for every single page. Helpfully, then, Apache can generate its own indexes automatically. For instance, if you create a directory called /var/www/tmp and drop some random files into it, then go to http://127.0.0.1/tmp in your web browser, you'll see a display similar to this:

Apache will generate index listings of files automatically.

In the absence of an index.html file, Apache will show the contents of a directory in a listing format, so you can download what you want. If you don't want Apache to show the contents of a directory, just give it a bare index.html file like this:

```
<html>
</html>
```

Once you've constructed your website, you'll want to share it with the rest of the world. The first thing you'll need to do is make sure that network port 80 – the standard web-serving port – is not being blocked by your router or modem. (Consult your router/modem documentation to check this. If you have multiple machines connected to a router, make sure the router is forwarding port 80 to your Linux box.) Next you'll need to find out your Internet-facing IP address, so go to www. whatsmyip.org or Google 'what is my IP' to find out. This is the number used to identify your machine on the Internet.

Prefix your IP address with 'http://' and you have the address that you can give people to browse your website, eg 'http://209.85.227.105'. Of course, this will only work while your PC is booted, and your ISP might give you a different IP address each time you power on your router/modem. If you want a more permanent web presence for your PC, talk to your ISP about getting a static IP address and a domain name.

You can use your locally hosted website to test compatibility with other OSes and browsers on your local network. To find out your local network IP address of the Linux box (which is different to the Internet-facing address that your router/modem has), enter this on your Linux machine:

```
ifconfig | grep 'inet addr'
```

Choose the IP address next to 'inet addr:' that's not 127.0.0.1 (this is covered in more detail in the SSH server section, earlier). Once you have determined the address, you can use it to access your Linux machine's Apache installation from another system on your network.

Here we're testing the Linux-hosted site in Safari on a Mac. No browser compatibility problems here! Granted, it is a very simple site. . . .

ADVANCED LINUX
Your own BitTorrent tracker

Y ou've probably already heard of BitTorrent: it's the most popular way to share large files on the Internet. BitTorrent is a peer-to-peer (P2P) network, which means that files aren't hosted on any single specific server, but instead many users around the Internet share the files using their BitTorrent programs. If you use BitTorrent to get a file, you'll download chunks of it from various computers on the P2P network – so the more people that are sharing a file, the faster it is to download.

This does mean that BitTorrent is often used to pirate software and films, as there's no single website or file server that the authorities can take down, but it's also great for sharing (legitimate!) large files such as Linux distributions. You could

BitTorrent

BitTorrent is a peer-to-peer download network that sometimes enables higher download speeds and more reliable downloads of large files. You will need to install a Bit Torrent client on your computer in order to enable this download method. You may then use one of the following links to download the Ubuntu cd image:

Ubuntu 9.10

- ubuntu-9.10-alternate-amd64.iso.torrent
- ubuntu-9.10-alternate-i386.iso.torrent
- ubuntu-9.10-desktop-amd64.iso.torrent
- ubuntu-9.10-desktop-i386.iso.torrent
- ubuntu-9.10-server-amd64.iso.torrent
- ubuntu-9.10-server-i386.iso.torrent
- **New:** IPv6 only torrents for users of IPv6 (learn more about IPv6)

Ubuntu 8.04

- ubuntu-8.04.4-alternate-amd64.iso.torrent

Ubuntu's website offers BitTorrent downloads as an option too.

Category	Age	Torrent Tags, Name		Size	S	L
Apps	129.5w	mandriva-linux-2008-one-KDE-cdrom-i586	+4★10⚑	694.09 MB	425	258
Apps	21.5w	mandriva-linux-free-2010.0-i586	+3★2⚑	4.26 GB	430	158
TV	111.1w	Linux CBT NUGGETS LINUX SERIES (VIDEO TUTORIAL).7z	+3★4⚑	1.42 GB	83	25
Apps	1.3w	Applications linux-praud-beta910v1.1	0⚑	2.14 GB	2	2
Books TorrentBox Verified	185.1w	130 linux and unix ebooks	+4★0⚑	1.11 GB	28	15
Apps	21.5w	mandriva-linux-one-2010.0-KDE4-europe1-americas-cdrom-i586	0⚑	678.11 MB	198	28
Apps	1.3w	Applications linux-praud-beta910v1.1.zip	0⚑	2.12 GB	1	0
Apps isoHunt Release	21.5w	[DL] mandriva-linux-free-2010.0-x86 64 [REL] mandriva-linux-free-2010.0-x86_64	0⚑	4.3 GB	166	36
Apps	1.1w	Sabayon Linux 5.2 x86 G.iso	0⚑	1.64 GB	67	12
Apps	1.1w	Sabayon Linux 5.2 x86 K.iso	0⚑	1.9 GB	58	15
Books	1.2w	Computers Beginning Ubuntu Linux 4th Ed. 2009	0⚑	17.35 MB	5	0

Sites like www.isohunt.com are often used to share Linux distributions.

make your own distro and share it via BitTorrent without having to spend huge amounts of money on bandwidth – imagine thousands of people pulling a 700MB file from your server if your distro becomes popular!

Most people share files using public 'trackers' on the Internet. These trackers are effectively central coordinating points for BitTorrent downloaders, providing information on the file and statistics for how many people are downloading and sharing ('seeding'). They don't actually contain any parts of the files themselves. It's not difficult to set up your own private BitTorrent tracker, running on your own machine, as we'll see now.

1 Install BitTorrent
First, we need to install BitTorrent. Open up a terminal and enter:

```
sudo apt-get install bittorrent
```

You may be prompted for your password. This command installs the command line BitTorrent software used to download files and run the tracker. When the tracker is running, it creates a couple of files used to describe what it's doing – they're files that you can check if something appears to be functioning incorrectly. Consequently, it's a good idea to make a new directory to run the tracker in:

```
mkdir mytracker
cd mytracker
```

```
mike@mike-laptop: ~
File Edit View Terminal Help
mike@mike-laptop:~$ sudo apt-get install bittorrent
[sudo] password for mike:
Reading package lists... Done
Building dependency tree
Reading state information... Done
The following extra packages will be installed:
  python-bittorrent
Suggested packages:
  bittorrent-gui
The following NEW packages will be installed
  bittorrent python-bittorrent
0 upgraded, 2 newly installed, 0 to remove and 520 not upgraded.
Need to get 107kB of archives.
After this operation, 651kB of additional disk space will be used.
Do you want to continue [Y/n]? y
Get: 1 http://gb.archive.ubuntu.com/ubuntu/ lucid/main python-bittorrent 3.4.2-1
1.1ubuntu4 [53.2kB]
Get: 2 http://gb.archive.ubuntu.com/ubuntu/ lucid/main bittorrent 3.4.2-11.1ubun
tu4 [54.0kB]
Fetched 107kB in 0s (346kB/s)
Selecting previously deselected package python-bittorrent.
(Reading database ... 122685 files and directories currently installed.)
Unpacking python-bittorrent (from .../python-bittorrent_3.4.2-11.1ubuntu4_all.de
b) ...
```

2 Run the tracker

Here's the command to run to start it:

```
bttrack --port 6969 --dfile dstate
    --logfile tracker.log
```

The BitTorrent tracker is written in the Python programming language so you might see a couple of Python warnings, but you can ignore them. Now our tracker is up and running on network port 6969 on our computer: it's not doing anything yet, as we've not associated it with any BitTorrent downloads.

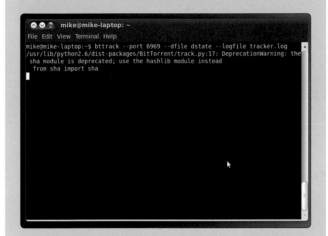

3 Check that it's OK

You can check that it's working by visiting http://127.0.0.1:6969 in your web browser – remember that 127.0.0.1 is the network address of your local machine. (Indeed, any address starting with 127.x.x.x is used for the local machine – no need to worry, you won't accidentally access someone's random machine on the internet!) If it's all working correctly, you'll see a result similar to that in the screenshot below.

4 Create a metafile

In order to share a file, we need to create a .torrent 'metafile' file for it: this is a file that tells BitTorrent programs which tracker they need to locate, how the chunks of the file fit together and so forth. It doesn't contain any of the file itself. In this example we have a file called 'dsl-4.4.10.iso', which is an ISO image of Damn Small Linux, a Linux distribution.

As we'll be sharing it over the net, we need to find out our IP address so that other BitTorrent programs can connect to our tracker. Visit www.whatsmyip.org (or Google 'what is my IP') to discover it, and then open a new terminal window and run this command:

```
btmakemetafile filename
    http://<IP address>:6969/announce
```

Replace filename with the file from which you want to generate a .torrent, and <IP address> with your real address. In our example the

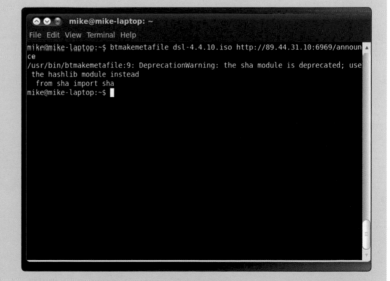

command is 'btmakemetafile dsl-4.4.10.iso http://89.44.31.10:6969/announce'.

This creates a file called 'dsl-4.4.10.iso. torrent', which is the small metafile containing information about the full, original file.

Sharing with the world

So let's recap: we have our own BitTorrent tracker running, and now we have a .torrent file for a Linux distribution. We could hand out that .torrent file to anyone we want – send it by email, or put it on a web server as described in the previous section. However, there are a couple of things we need to do beforehand.

Firstly, we need to ensure that all of the necessary network ports are available to the outside world. Using your modem or router's configuration panel (consult the device's documentation if you don't know how to access it), make sure that port 6969 – the port that the tracker is using – is accessible to the outside world. In many routers with multiple machines connected you'll need to look at the 'port forwarding' part.

Secondly, we need to start seeding the file ourselves. Right now, nobody is sharing the dsl-4.4.10.iso file from which we've made the .torrent – so even if you gave the .torrent to everyone in the world, nobody could get the full file. Someone, somewhere needs to be sharing the full version of the file using their BitTorrent software, so that others can get parts of it and start sharing in turn.

We can kick off this chain reaction. Enter:

```
sudo apt-get install rtorrent
```

This is a BitTorrent program – the normal type of downloading program that most people use. Enter 'rtorrent' and you'll see this screen:

Installing the 'rtorrent' BitTorrent client.

Running 'rtorrent' for the first time.

It's largely empty because we're not uploading or sharing anything yet. Hit the backspace key, and you'll see a 'load_start' prompt appear at the bottom: this is asking you for the name of a .torrent file. You can hit Tab to see a list of files above.

rtorrent requesting the name of a .torrent file.

Type in the name of the .torrent file – eg dsl-4.4.10.iso.torrent – and you'll see that it appears in the rtorrent list like this:

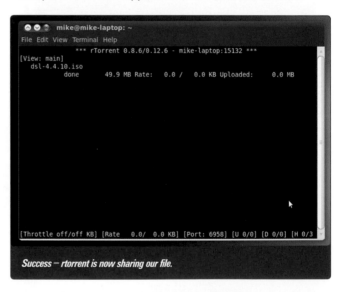

Success – rtorrent is now sharing our file.

rtorrent looks for dsl-4.4.10.iso (it needs to be in the current directory) and then starts sharing it. We are now 'seeding' the full file to the world, so anyone who gets hold of our dsl-4.4.10. iso.torrent file can open it in their BitTorrent program. Their program will read the .torrent file and discover various bits of info: 'Aha, the full file is called dsl-4.4.10.iso, and the tracker is located at http://82.44.31.10:6969/announce. I will connect to the tracker and find out who is sharing the file.'

On connecting to the tracker, their program will discover that we are sharing the file using our 'rtorrent' program, which just happens to be on the same server as the tracker. Once they start downloading the file, they will automatically start sharing it too, and send that information back to the tracker. So ultimately, as more and more people download the file, more and more people will be sharing it too, making the downloads more reliable.

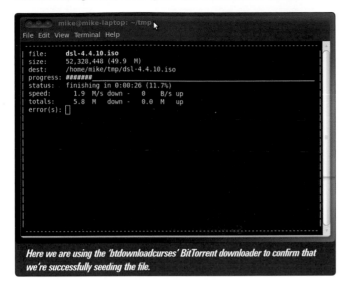

Here we are using the 'btdownloadcurses' BitTorrent downloader to confirm that we're successfully seeding the file.

Opening the right ports

There's one last bit of port work we need to do before we go live: BitTorrent operates on ports 6881 to 6999. For most cases, however, you only need to make sure that ports 6881 to 6889 are open, so set them as accessible in your modem/router's options screen as described earlier.

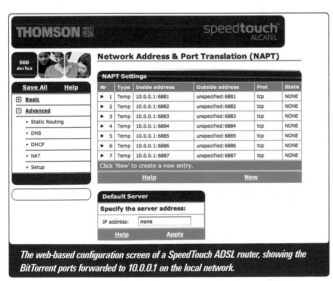

The web-based configuration screen of a SpeedTouch ADSL router, showing the BitTorrent ports forwarded to 10.0.0.1 on the local network.

So, in all you now have two terminals running: one contains the tracker, providing coordination information for all the BitTorrent activity; and the other contains rtorrent, serving up the first instance of the file. You'll want to leave these running for as long as you want to run the tracker or serve files. If you want to serve another file, simply run 'btmakemetafile' with it as described earlier, then go to the rtorrent terminal, hit

backspace and enter the filename of the resulting .torrent. You can look at tracker.log in the mytracker directory you created at the start if you suspect that anything isn't working properly.

Limiting bandwidth

rtorrent lets you limit the upload rate – useful if a file becomes popular and is saturating your connection. In the rtorrent terminal, look in the bottom-left corner at the 'Throttle' status line and press 'a' (lower-case). The number on the left will increase – that's the upload rate, in kilobytes per second. You can keep raising it with 'a', or lower it with 'z'. For a typical home DSL connection, you shouldn't need to have it set above 20 when other people are sharing the same file via your tracker.

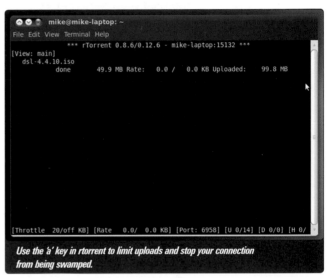

Use the 'a' key in rtorrent to limit uploads and stop your connection from being swamped.

Enter 'man bttrack' to see what else you can do with the tracker (including operating on different ports and IP addresses), and 'man rtorrent' for information on the BitTorrent client. See www.bittorrent.com, the official home page of BitTorrent, and www.btfaq.com for useful information on trackers and clients.

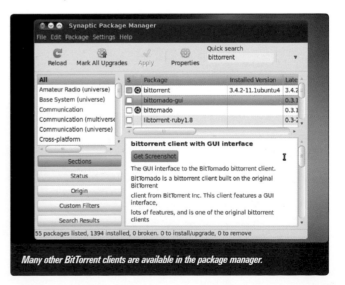

Many other BitTorrent clients are available in the package manager.

Programming

08.

In this section

PROGRAMMING
Importance of programming

In a typical software company, the development process goes like this:

1 The company hires a bunch of coders.
2 Coders work on a product for money, whether they like the project or not.
3 The company releases the product when it thinks it can make the most money.

As we've seen, money doesn't play such a big role in the Free Software world. Indeed, for many of the programmers working on Linux money doesn't even come into the equation; it's all about the love and challenge of working on something so special. Linux would certainly survive if all of the unpaid developers dropped out, but it would run the risk of morphing into any other random commercial project with bored programmers and release dates decided by the marketing department (no matter how many bugs remain).

So, the more hobbyist, for-the-love-of-it developers that Linux can attract, the better. Great new ideas can appear from the laptop of a spare-time coder sitting in his garden. A random university student may discover a completely new way of doing a task in the Linux kernel, thereby speeding up the OS for everyone on the planet. Because Linux is totally open, anyone can make a huge difference to the future of computing.

Free Software developers often meet up in person for intensive programming sessions known as 'hackfests'. (Photo: CC-SA, mariosp on Flickr)

Now, if you've never written a line of code before in your life, you might find all of this somewhat daunting. Coding is not a black art, though. This author started programming in BASIC on the ZX Spectrum in 1988, when he was eight years old. Most other developers got started in the same way – not by poring over dusty algorithms or spending years in a dreary programming school. No, they did it instead by exploring their computers, taking other people's code and seeing what they could do with it.

Sure, tackling a mammoth project such as an office suite requires years of experience, but programming small utilities and games is within the reach of everyone. It's fun, stimulating and gets you on the road to becoming a Linux developer.

Here we're going to sample Python, one of the most friendly and readable programming languages in existence. But by no means is it just for beginners – Python is included with most Linux distributions and many notable apps are written in it, such as the installation program you used to install Ubuntu!

If you've programmed in another language before, some of the concepts introduced here won't be new to you, but take this as an opportunity to get acquainted with Python. Note that Python is available for many other operating systems, including Windows, and the skills you'll learn here are applicable to other programming languages as well.

Sinclair's 8-bit ZX Spectrum was a major success in the 1980s and introduced the BASIC programming language to millions. (Photo: CC-SA, Bill Bertram)

PROGRAMMING
First steps with Python

Close any windows cluttering up your desktop, and then open two programs: a text editor (Applications > Accessories > gEdit) and a command line window (Applications > Accessories > Terminal). We're going to write our Python programs in the text editor, and run them in the terminal. (Quick tip: use Alt+Tab to switch between the two programs without having to grab the mouse.)

In the text editor, write:

```
print "Hello, planet!"
```

and save the file in your home directory as myprog.py. Switch to the terminal window and enter 'python myprog.py' to see the result:

```
Hello, planet!
```

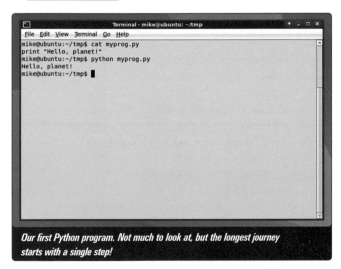

Our first Python program. Not much to look at, but the longest journey starts with a single step!

Congratulations – you've written your first Python program. (You now also have more programming experience than most IT managers, but that's another matter.) What we're doing here is very simple: Python is an interpreted language, in that it reads each line of a text file and executes it. You don't need to compile anything to machine code.

When we run 'python myprog.py', the Python interpreter loads our text file and starts executing the first line. 'Ah', it says, 'there's a print command. I'll print the text following it.' When Python reaches the end of the file – after the first line in our case – it closes the file and stops execution, putting you back at the command prompt.

Playing with variables
Let's try something more complex. Type this in, save it and run 'python myprog.py' again:

```
x = 50
y = 10

print "x is", x
print "y is", y

z = x + y

print "x + y is", z
```

Variables are a core part of almost any program – here we're assigning them some numbers.

In this program we're introducing 'variables'. As the name suggests, these things can vary: they are storage units for numbers that can change throughout the course of the program. In the first two lines we tell Python that we want two of these storage pigeon-holes, called x and y. (You can give variables almost any name – myvar, score, height etc.)

We also tell Python that we want the x variable to store 50, and the y variable to store 10. We can change the contents of these variables at any time later on. But first we want to confirm that they're definitely, absolutely storing the right values, so we print them out on the following two lines. We could just say 'print x' to print the number that x contains, but it's nice to provide a bit of text before. Text must be surrounded by double-quote characters, and we separate it from the variable name with a comma.

So, we see that x is definitely 50 and y is 10. Next we perform an arithmetic operation: we create a new variable, z, and tell it to store the result of x and y added together. Python lets you do a range of operations on numbers and variables:

```
z = x + y
z = x - y - 6
z = x * 500
z = y / 30
```

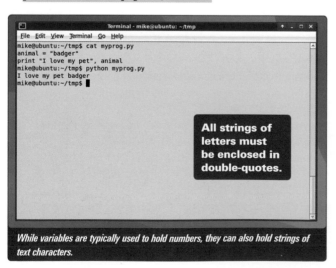

Variables are ultra-flexible – you can add, subtract, multiply and divide as much as you want.

The asterisk is used for multiplication, and the slash ('/') character is used for division. In our program we're performing a simple addition command and printing the result.

Variables as strings

Variables don't just have to hold numbers, though – you can create variables to hold strings of letters. Enter and run this program:

```
animal = "badger"
print "I love my pet", animal
```

All strings of letters must be enclosed in double-quotes.

While variables are typically used to hold numbers, they can also hold strings of text characters.

■ Getting input from the user

Most programs need to do more than deal with the numbers and strings they contain – they need to get more data from the outside world. Let's make Python ask for keyboard input from the user. Run this program:

```
result = raw_input("Enter your name: ")
print "Wow! My cat is called", result, "too!"
```

This small program introduces several features of Python. We create a variable called result as per usual, but this time, instead of directly giving it a number or string to hold we tell it to store the results of an operation called raw_input().

This raw_input() is called a function: it refers to a subroutine, a piece of code stored elsewhere in the Python interpreter's files. We don't have to know where raw_input() is or how it works – we only need to know that it exists, and that we can use it whenever we want. This function prints a string of text to the screen, and then waits for the user to type in something and press Enter. When the user hits Enter, the typed-in string is sent back and stored in the variable before the equals sign ('result' in our case).

What are the brackets for? These keep together the bits of information that we send to the raw_input() function. In our program, we're sending it one piece of information, the 'Enter your name' string. Some functions need multiple bits of information – known as arguments or parameters, and they are separated inside the brackets with commas. You'll see more examples of this later.

So, this program asks the user to enter a word, and then prints a message of surprise with the 'result' variable squeezed in between. We use raw_input() to get strings of letters from the user, and input() for numbers:

```
x = input("Enter a number: ")
y = input("Enter another: ")
print "Added together they are", x + y
```

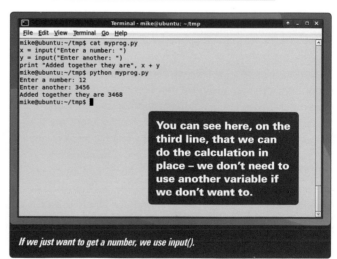

You can see here, on the third line, that we can do the calculation in place – we don't need to use another variable if we don't want to.

If we just want to get a number, we use input().

■ Controlling program flow

In very simple programs a linear set of instructions will suffice, but if we want to do anything more complex we'll need to make decisions based on the results of certain actions. We do this using the 'if' instruction, which performs an action (or sequence of actions) if a certain condition is met. Look at this program:

```
x = input("Enter a number: ")

if (x == 10):
    print "You entered ten!"
```

Here we get a number from the user, and then perform an 'if' comparison. Notice that there are two equals signs here – this is very important! If we just used 'x = 10' then that is simply putting the number 10 into the x variable. We don't want that; we want to perform a comparison. So 'x == 10' (two equals signs) says 'If x is equal to 10 . . .'

The 'if' operation is surrounded by brackets and followed by a colon. What happens next is fundamental to the workings of Python. You'll see that the 'print' line is indented – ie pushed forward with a tab. Indentation marks chunks of code that depend on a bigger, 'mother' instruction. In this case, any instructions after the 'if' line that are indented by a tab will be executed if the 'if' comparison works. So, you can have:

```
if (x == 10):
    print "This will be executed if x is 10"
    print "And this too..."
    print "And this!"

print "But this bit will be printed regardless."
print "There is no more indentation, so this"
print "part doesn't depend on the if above"
```

Indentation is used heavily throughout Python as a way of denoting which bits of code relate to certain instructions.

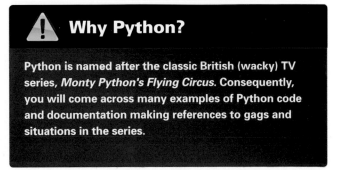

Indentation is crucially important for Python to know which instructions belong to which bit of the code.

Types of comparisons

With 'if' we can perform all manner of comparisons:

```
if (x > 10):
if (x < 10):
if (x != 10):
if (x >= 10):
```

In order, these are: if x is greater than ten; if x is less than ten; if x is not equal to ten; and if x is greater than or equal to ten. Now, if we want a certain action to be performed if the condition doesn't match, we can use 'else' like this:

```
if (x == 10):
    print "You entered ten!"
else:
    print "Not ten, in fact"
```

All indented code beneath the 'else' block will be executed if the previous 'if' condition doesn't match. Note that you can put multiple 'if' instructions inside one another, providing that you keep using indentation:

```
if (x == 10):
    if (y > 5):
        print "x is ten and y is bigger than 5"
```

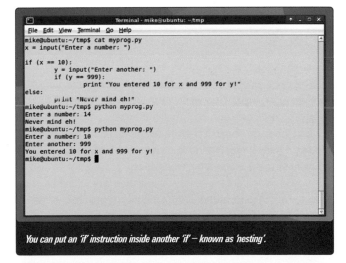

You can put an 'if' instruction inside another 'if' – known as 'nesting'.

⚠ Why Python?

Python is named after the classic British (wacky) TV series, *Monty Python's Flying Circus*. Consequently, you will come across many examples of Python code and documentation making references to gags and situations in the series.

Repeating operations with loops

Let's move on to loops. Very often you'll want to perform an action more than once – indeed, perhaps hundreds of times. It'd be insanely laborious (and resource-wasting) to copy-and-paste your code so many times, so we use loops to help us out. Essentially, a loop says: 'Execute the following set of instructions while a certain condition is true.' For this we use the 'while' instruction like so:

```
x = 0

while (x < 10):
    print x
    x = x + 1
```

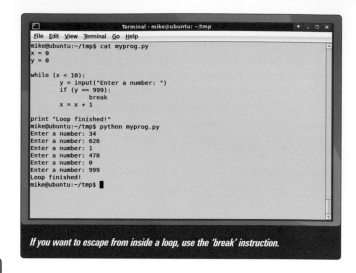

If you want to escape from inside a loop, use the 'break' instruction.

Loops let you repeat code multiple times, or even for infinity if required.

When you run this program, you'll see that it prints out numbers from 0 to 9. Our 'while' loop is saying: 'While the variable x contains a number smaller than ten, print out the value of x and then add one to it.' Again, the indentation is massively important here: when Python finds no more indented code, it jumps back to the start of the 'while' loop.

If you didn't indent the 'x = x + 1' line then it wouldn't be executed in the loop, and therefore the loop would run forever. That's called an infinite loop. (Tip: to escape from infinite loops press Ctrl+c to get back to the command prompt.)

We can force a 'while' loop to end using the 'break' instruction:

```
x = 0
y = 0

while (x < 10):
    y = input("Enter a number: ")
    if (y == 999):
        break
    x = x + 1

print "Loop finished!"
```

In this program, we set off with the intention of running the 'while' loop ten times, as before. But each time the loop is executed, we ask the user for a number. If the user enters 999, the 'break' instruction is executed and we jump to the final 'print' line. Conversely, if the user enters any other number, the loop continues as before.

■ Save time – reuse your code

Loops save a lot of typing and keep a program's code small, but they're not the only way to improve efficiency. Earlier we mentioned 'functions', neatly wrapped-up chunks of code that you can reuse again and again without having to type it in multiple times. Here's an example of a function being created and used:

```
def showhelp():
    print "Here is some help text."
    print "Blah foo sausage banana"
    print "purple monkey dishwasher"

showhelp()
print "Ending program!"
```

Functions let you quickly and easily reuse parts of your code.

In the first line of this program, we use 'def' to define a new function called 'showhelp'. (We'll explain what the brackets are for in a moment.) After the name of the function has been defined, we type the code that we want executed when the function is run – indented, of course. In this case, our function merely prints three lines of text, but it can do anything you want.

Note that defining a function doesn't execute it; it merely tells Python that it exists. You need to define functions before you run them, so it's always best to put them at the start of the program. So, program execution begins after the function definition with the 'showhelp()' instruction. This runs – or 'calls' – our function, and when the function has finished (when the indented code runs out) it goes back to the main code and executes the final 'print' line.

Functions will save you enormous amounts of time as you write more and more code. Say you're writing a large program, and it has various places in which the user can view the help text. If you didn't use a function like we've done here, you'd have to paste the help-text-showing code into multiple places. Then imagine that you wanted to implement a new feature in your program – or change the way something works. Without a function, you'd have to painstakingly go through your program, making sure that all the help text bits were correct and up to date. With a function, however, you have the text in a single place, so you only have to make the changes there.

Now, a moment ago we referred to the brackets used in the function definition. For a function that just prints text, we don't need anything inside those brackets. But for more versatile functions, we can send numbers to them and retrieve numbers from them. Try this program.

```
def doubler(num):
    result = num * 2
    return result

x = input("Enter a number ")
y = doubler(x)
print "Doubled, that is", y
```

Here we define a function called doubler, and inside the brackets we create a new variable called 'num'. This function is saying: 'When you call me, you can also send me a number which I will store in a variable called num.' (Of course, you can give the variable another name if you wish.)

Inside this function we create a new variable called 'result' and give it the value of 'num' multiplied by two. We then use an instruction called 'return', which sends back a number to the code that called the function. But how do we send numbers to a function and get numbers back? This is done in this line of our program:

You can send the contents of variables to functions and get numbers back from them too.

```
y = doubler(x)
```

Here, we call our 'doubler' function, sending the contents of the x variable as a number. (The 'doubler' function then stores that number in its own variable, 'num', as we saw.) When the function executes the 'return' command, it finishes execution and sends the number back, and is stored into whatever variable we put before the equals sign. So here, y contains whatever was 'returned' by the 'doubler' function.

You can create functions that let you send – or 'pass' – multiple numbers to them, with the variables separated by commas:

```
def addnumbers(num1, num2):
    result = num1 + num2
    return result

x = addnumbers(50, 9000)
print x
```

This will print '9050' to the screen.

Functions can take multiple variables, which are also known as parameters.

Notice that variables live inside the current chunk of code, and can't be overwritten by other functions for safety reasons. Consider this:

```
def test():
        x = 50
        print x


x = 2300
test()
print x
```

Note that functions use their own, local versions of variables, so they don't interfere with the main (calling) code.

When you run this, you'll see the number 50 and then 2300 on the screen. The reason is simple: in the main program we set the variable x to be 2300, and when we call the 'test' function it creates its own x variable that doesn't overwrite or affect the number in the main code. This lets you create functions with any variable names you want, safe in the knowledge that they won't stomp all over variables anywhere else in your program!

■ Make your own admin tools

We've explored quite a lot of the Python language, so let's wrap it up with a serious program: a system administration menu that can be modified to do whatever you want. First, though, let's look at a way to execute command line programs on the system from within Python. Run this program:

```
from os import system
system('ls')
```

This runs the 'ls' program to display a list of files (see the Advanced Linux section for more information on command line programs). As you can see, we use a function called 'system' to execute commands.

Using the system() command you can run any program on your Linux installation.

However, 'system' isn't available in the absolute core of Python, so we have to 'import' it from an external bunch of code called 'os'. That's what the first line does – you will see 'import' used in other programs that depend on external libraries of functions.

Type in and run this program:

```
from os import system


def showoptions():
        print "SYSTEM ADMIN PANEL 1.0"
        print ""
        print "1 - Quit"
        print "2 - Delete a file"
        print "3 - Show disk info"
        print ""


def deletefile():
        filename = raw_input("Enter filename: ")
        result = system("rm " + filename)
        if (result != 0):
                print "Error deleting file!"
        else:
                print "File deleted OK"
        print "Press enter..."
        raw_input()


def diskinfo():
        system("df -h")
        print "Press enter..."
        raw_input()


x = 0


while (x != 1):
        system("clear")
```

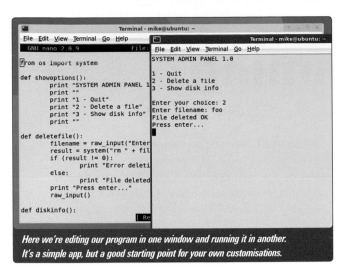

Here we're editing our program in one window and running it in another. It's a simple app, but a good starting point for your own customisations.

```
showoptions()
x = input("Enter your choice: ")

if (x == 2):
        deletefile()
if (x == 3):
        diskinfo()

print "Program ended."
```

A quick run-through: we define three functions, and then program execution begins at the 'x = 0' point. Then we have a loop in which we clear the screen, ask the user for a number and then perform the appropriate action. If the user enters '2' we call our file deletion routine, which contains this line:

```
result = system('rm ' + filename)
```

As you can see with the plus (+) sign, we can join together two strings of characters. So if the user has

entered 'file1.txt', the command we end up running is 'rm file1.txt'. Notice that 'system()' returns a number: it's zero if the command executed correctly, or not zero if there's a problem – eg the file doesn't exist or we don't have the right permissions. We look at that number (in the 'result' variable) and show an appropriate message.

This program is very simple, but it's a starting point for you to customise and make your own administration tools. For instance, you could create an option to restart the Apache web server, or make a backup of your home directory. The best thing to do is experiment! There's so much more to explore in Python – see www.python.org/doc/ for links to more guides and reference material.

Happy coding!

■ Further resources

Having learnt something about programming in Python, you may want to increase your knowledge further, and there are various online resources available to help you do this:

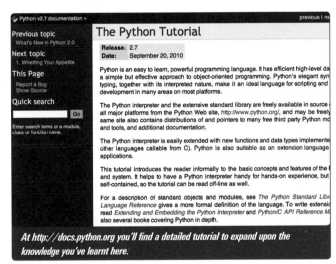

At http://docs.python.org you'll find a detailed tutorial to expand upon the knowledge you've learnt here.

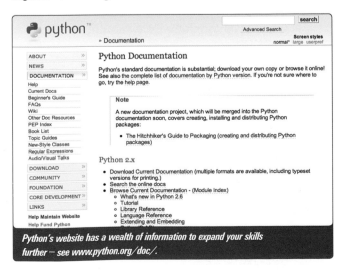

Python's website has a wealth of information to expand your skills further – see www.python.org/doc/.

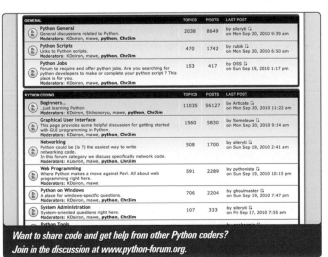

Want to share code and get help from other Python coders? Join in the discussion at www.python-forum.org.

PROGRAMMING
Good programming

Here are a few things to bear in mind when you're programming. By far and away the most important is to make your code readable. Use variable names that make sense – such as 'score' rather than 's' or 'timeout' rather than 't'. There's no performance penalty for using longer variable names, and it will help if you later come back to a piece of code that you haven't touched for a while. One of the most common mistakes that everyone makes in programming (even experienced programmers are guilty!) is to write a large chunk of code in a frenzy of inspiration, only to look at it a few days later and have absolutely no idea what's going on. Therefore it's a very good idea to include lots of comments in your code; in Python these start with a hash mark like this:

```
# This routine saves the image to disk
def diskinfo():
    print "Saving file..."
    ...
```

It's better to have more comments than necessary, rather than none at all. And, of course, well-chosen variable names and good comments make it easier for others to work with your code, if you ever decide to share it with the world.

Don't try to optimise your program too soon. Yes, the performance of a program is important, but in the early stages of development an aggressive performance target can lead to major problems down the road. Donald Knuth, one of the most respected programmers of all time, said that 'premature optimisation is the root of all evil'. As you're creating the program, design should be the most important consideration – how the code fits together, keeping things modular so that one function can't break another one, looking for the best technical solutions rather than quick fixes. You may be able to rewrite a piece of code so that it's 10% faster, but if it makes it much harder to modify the routine later to add new features, it's not the best approach!

If your program gets to the state where you'd like to look for outside involvement, there are many options available. The best approach is to choose an open source project hosting provider: these give you a bit of webspace for your files and various extras like bug reporting systems, forums, download counters and so forth. The most popular is www.sourceforge.net, which holds thousands of projects but suffers from the occasional slowdown; so alternatives such as www.berlios.de are worth considering too. These sites are free to sign up to; they exist to help the open source community.

Of course, before you create a webpage you'll need a name for your project. Linux programs tend to have quirky names such as Banshee and Pidgin; on the one hand these names are hard to forget, but on the other they don't tell you anything about what the software does. You could opt for a more generic name – eg BlipEditor for a text editor – but be careful about using names similar to commercial software. Some years ago a project was set up called KIllustrator, providing a vector graphics editing tool. Adobe caught wind of this and pointed out that the name could suggest that it was some variant of Adobe Illustrator. Wanting to avoid costly legal battles, the KIllustrator team duly changed the name.

Once you have your website designed, upload the first release of your code. At this point nobody will know that your application exists, so go to http://freshmeat.net, register an account (it's free) and post an entry telling the world about your work. Freshmeat is a constantly updating index of free software releases – many people read it, so if someone likes what you're doing they'll be tempted to join in.

To get people involved, set up a forum or mailing list on your hosting provider. In the early days of a project there's a tendency for everyone to get bogged down with grand design decisions and visions of the future, so try to keep your co-developers focused on the tasks in hand. Some developers may claim that they're going to add features X, Y and Z to your program, and then disappear forever; that's just one of the by-products of a free and open development community. But hopefully you'll gradually build up a solid team, getting new releases out of the door and finding recognition for your work.

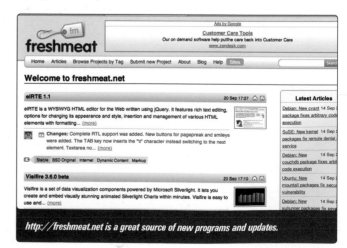

PROGRAMMING
Contributing to projects

Helping out with free software development is a brilliant way to contribute back to the community. If you're a seasoned developer, you can provide support by adding new features and fixing bugs. Many projects provide version control systems for the source code, allowing you to be constantly up to date with the latest changes. Hunt around on a project's website for information on SVN or CVS access – failing that, find the lead developer's email address or a mailing list and see what you can get.

Many free software projects are developed in two separate branches. One is typically called 'stable' and is the place where only bug fixes and security patches are added – nothing else changes. The (more exciting) branch where new features are implemented, and old, stale features ripped out, is usually called 'current'. If you plan to add a new feature to a program or make some large under-the-hood changes, you'll want to do it in the current branch.

If you can't help out with a project from the coding side, there are many other ways to get involved. A lot

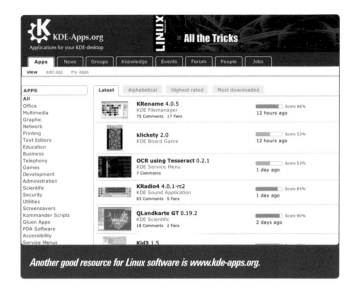

Another good resource for Linux software is www.kde-apps.org.

of free software has quite terse documentation, geared towards other developers rather than end users. If you find a program that doesn't have a decent user manual, you could write one and mail it to the developers.

Another option is artwork: if you find a program that looks horribly bland and could do with a lick of paint, fire up Gimp and create new icons, splash screens etc. (This is particularly true for games.)

Simplest of all, you can sign up to the website forums or mailing list of a program or a distro and provide help to other users if they get stuck. When the community works together this way – with people helping one another and chipping in with their own talents – then nothing can hold it back.

GETTING INVOLVED

Intention

GIMP is Free Software and a part of the GNU Project. In the free software world, there is generally no distinction between users and developers. As in a friendly neighbourhood, everybody pitches in to help their neighbors. Please consider the time you give in assistance to others as payment.

Ways in which you can help:

- program new features,
- report bugs (errors in the program),
- debug existing features,
- add documentation,
- translate GIMP to your own language,
- translate the documentation,
- write tutorials,
- participate in the UI brainstorm,
- improve this web site,
- make artwork for GIMP used in or with GIMP,
- let people know you used GIMP for your artwork,
- give away copies of GIMP,
- help others to learn to use GIMP, etc.

As you can see, everyone can help.

Gimp (www.gimp.org/develop/) has pages showing the various ways in which you can get involved.

PROGRAMMING
Programming languages

Almost any programming language you can name has some form of implementation on Linux. Here we'll go through some of the most notable ones:

C/C++

C is the standard low-level systems programming language: almost all of the Linux kernel is written in C. It sees some use on the desktop in Gnome and its apps, although KDE, Firefox, OpenOffice.org and other large projects are written in C++. The de facto standard C/C++ compiler for Linux is GCC, the GNU Compiler Collection (http://gcc.gnu.org). A particularly good integrated development environment, or IDE, is Anjuta (http://projects.gnome.org/anjuta/).

C#

A rather controversial language due to its origins in Microsoft's research labs, C# is a powerful programming language that's well supported on Linux thanks to the efforts of the Mono project (www.mono-project.com). The MonoDevelop IDE provides a great alternative to Microsoft's Visual Studio.

BASIC

If you're a fan of Visual BASIC or you grew up hacking 8-bit BASIC code on the ZX Spectrum or C64, you'll love Gambas (http://gambas.sourceforge.net). This is a complete development environment with a BASIC-like programming language for writing command line and graphical apps.

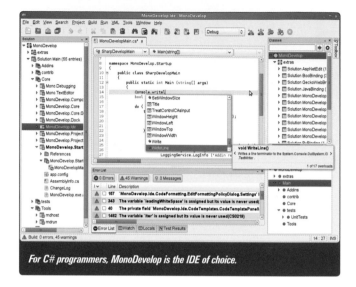

For C# programmers, MonoDevelop is the IDE of choice.

Pascal

Although it's mostly confined to education, there are some real-world uses of Pascal too. An excellent compiler for Linux is Free Pascal (www.freepascal.org).

Perl

One of the most powerful text processing languages in existence, Perl sees heavy use among administrators for quickly hacking together scripts. You can do a huge amount with Perl but sometimes the code is almost unreadable (www.perl.org).

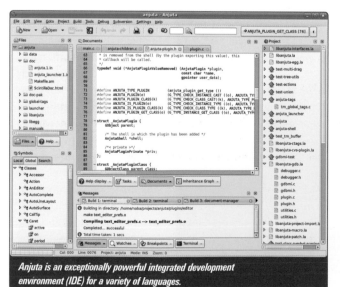

Anjuta is an exceptionally powerful integrated development environment (IDE) for a variety of languages.

If you've got experience with Visual BASIC on Windows, you'll feel right at home in Gambas.

Eclipse (www.eclipse.org) is one of the most popular Java IDEs, and it can be extended to other languages too.

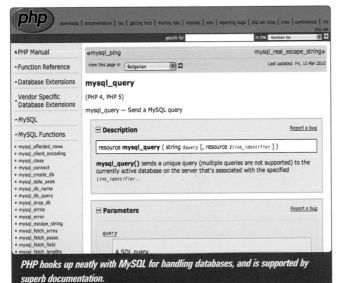

PHP hooks up neatly with MySQL for handling databases, and is supported by superb documentation.

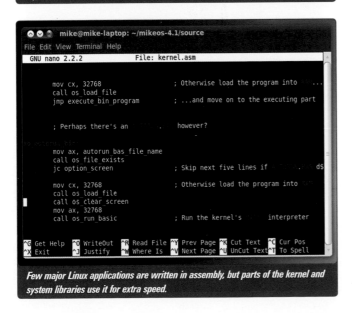

Few major Linux applications are written in assembly, but parts of the kernel and system libraries use it for extra speed.

Text editor

Note that while many languages don't have dedicated IDEs, the gEdit text editor supplied with Ubuntu includes syntax highlighting (keyword and variable colouring) for many languages. This makes code so much more readable and better on the eyes after long programming sessions. Another good editor for coding is jEdit, available at www.jedit.org and in Ubuntu's package manager.

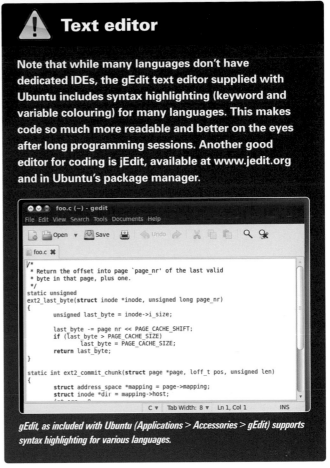

gEdit, as included with Ubuntu (Applications > Accessories > gEdit) supports syntax highlighting for various languages.

Java

The 'write once, run anywhere' language is well supported on Linux, with many applications and games built on it. The most popular Java implementation is from Sun/Oracle (www.java.com).

Ruby

A relatively new language, Ruby (www.ruby-lang.org) has taken off in recent years due to its use in Ruby on Rails, a website construction framework (www.rubyonrails.org).

PHP

Originally a set of scripts to make website development easier, PHP (www.php.net) is now one of the biggest server-side languages in the world. Many web applications from email clients to e-commerce solutions are written in PHP.

Assembly

If you want to get down to the bare metal of your machine, assembly language – human-readable mnemonics for machine-code instructions – is the way to go. NASM (www.nasm.us) is an especially good assembler, and you can find a full tutorial for assembly on Linux at http://asm.sf.net.

09.
Appendices

In this section

APPENDIX 1
Distributors of Linux

These are the 30 most popular distributions of Linux, as determined by the number of distro-specific page views on the DistroWatch.com website:

Ubuntu
www.ubuntu.com

The Linux distribution included with this book. Based on Debian, Ubuntu has separate desktop, server and netbook editions, and has many fans due to its clean, uncluttered desktop, excellent hardware detection and lively supporting community.

Fedora
www.fedoraproject.org

Backed by Red Hat, one of the biggest Linux companies, Fedora is a community-supported distro that aims to showcase the newest Linux technology. Many of the features that are pioneered in Fedora make their way into Red Hat Enterprise Linux.

Mint
www.linuxmint.com

Based on Ubuntu, Mint adds a different interface design along with some multimedia codecs (DVD and MP3 playback) that Ubuntu can't include due to software patent and copyright concerns. Mint has a busy community that's happy to accept new ideas.

OpenSUSE
www.opensuse.org

Originally known as SUSE Linux, one of the longest-running Linux distros, OpenSUSE is backed up by Novell and is famous for its powerful configuration system, YAST (Yet Another Setup Tool). It has a vast range of software in its repositories.

Mandriva
www.mandriva.com

Formerly known as Mandrake, Mandriva strives all-out to be friendly for Linux newcomers. It was one of the first distributions to feature a graphical installer, and today offers boxed set versions with support and extra features.

Debian GNU/Linux
www.debian.org

A favourite of long-time Linux users, Debian doesn't include lots of graphical setup tools and wizards, but it's extremely reliable and well tested. Releases are supported for several years, and consequently it's the basis for many other distros such as Ubuntu.

Sabayon
www.sabayonlinux.org

Geared towards advanced users, Sabayon is a live distro that helps you to install Gentoo Linux (see next page). It includes a wide variety of software and desktop environments, but assumes plenty of prior Linux knowledge.

Puppy
www.puppylinux.org

This is a lightweight Linux distro designed to give older machines a new purpose in life. Its minimum requirements are a Pentium 166 MHz CPU and 128MB of RAM – yet it manages to squeeze in a fully usable desktop with Internet tools and office software.

Arch
www.archlinux.org

Targeted at power users, Arch features a special software packaging system called 'pacman' which provides rolling updates. This means you only install Arch once, and then keep receiving new programs as they're available, rather than doing big upgrades every year or two.

PCLinuxOS
www.pclinuxos.com

Originally a spin-off of Mandriva, PCLinuxOS has matured into a powerful and popular distro in its own right. It's known for having a very friendly community and forums, although sometimes there are long waits between releases.

Slackware
www.slackware.com

This is the world's longest-running Linux distribution, with version 1.0 arriving in 1993. It includes a text-based installer and assumes you're very familiar with Linux. Popular amongst long time Linux fans who want total control over their systems.

MEPIS
www.mepis.org

Focused on home and business users, MEPIS is designed to provide everything you need for desktop and office computing straight after the installation. A spin-off called AntiX runs on older PCs with less RAM.

CentOS
www.centos.org

Built from the source code for Red Hat Enterprise Linux (RHEL), CentOS is targeted at businesses with many desktop PCs and servers, providing long-term support. Used by those who need an enterprise-level distro but don't need commercial support.

Tiny Core
www.tinycorelinux.com

The world's smallest graphical Linux distribution. Tiny Core weighs in at a mere 10MB, and includes a simple desktop environment from which you can launch a package manager and obtain more programs via the Internet. Good for setting up web kiosks.

Gentoo
www.gentoo.org

An extremely powerful and versatile distro for very experienced users. Gentoo users typically compile the software they need from scratch, using a system called Portage, for extra features and performance. It also has superb documentation.

Ultimate Edition
www.ultimateedition.info

A fork of Ubuntu. Whereas Ubuntu fits on to a single CD and doesn't include certain media codecs due to legal issues, Ultimate packs in a vast range of software, codecs and desktop effects. It's an intense, turbocharged Ubuntu.

Kubuntu
www.kubuntu.org

An official Ubuntu derivative, Kubuntu is supplied with the KDE desktop environment instead of Gnome, and therefore includes a range of KDE software. Otherwise it's almost identical to Ubuntu underneath.

Zenwalk
www.zenwalk.org

A popular lightweight distro, Zenwalk is based on Slackware but tries to provide a more welcoming desktop experience for new users. There's a Core edition for servers (no GUI included).

Vector
www.vectorlinux.com

Small and fast, Vector targets users who know which programs they need and the distro tries to be unobtrusive. Various versions are available with different desktops and software versions.

KNOPPIX
www.knoppix.com

One of the first live distros (running directly from a DVD), KNOPPIX has evolved into a power-user's toolkit for taking Linux on the go and fixing problems on broken operating system installations – Windows or Linux.

Dreamlinux
www.dreamlinux.com.br

Developed in Brazil, Dreamlinux is based on Debian and includes an exceptionally polished desktop design and theme. Versions are available with the GNOME and Xfce desktops.

Sidux
www.sidux.com

This distro is released approximately every three months and provides the latest mid-development snapshots of Debian. It's a quick and easy way to get a preview of the next Debian release.

CrunchBang
www.crunchbanglinux.org

Another variant of Ubuntu, CrunchBang is more oriented towards highly experienced Linux users. It includes a very minimal desktop and a selection of advanced applications.

Elive
www.elivecd.org

This Debian-based distribution is a showcase for Enlightenment, an extremely configurable and snazzy window manager. Enlightenment used to be one of the flagship projects in the Free Software world.

gOS
www.thinkgos.com

An early attempt to combine Internet applications with the Linux desktop, gOS tries to tightly integrate Google Mail, Google Docs, Blogger and other services with locally stored programs.

BackTrack
www.backtrack-linux.org

A merger of two older projects, Auditor Security Linux and WHAX, this distro is supplied with a collection of security and forensics tools. Used by many administrators to inspect networks and maintain security.

Xubuntu
www.xubuntu.org

Xubuntu is a flavour of Ubuntu with a different desktop, in this case the memory-friendly Xfce. It removes some heavy and demanding programs (such as OpenOffice.org) and replaces them with lighter equivalents (eg AbiWord and Gnumeric).

ClearOS
www.clearfoundation.com

Based on CentOS, ClearOS is a network and gateway server distribution for small businesses. It includes software for blocking viruses and spam, filtering content and analysing log files.

TinyMe
www.tinymelinux.com

A small, light distribution based on Unity Linux. This distro is intended for use on older machines where only the 'bare essentials' are needed.

Ubuntu Studio
www.ubuntustudio.org

Another Ubuntu re-spin, Ubuntu Studio is targeted firmly at audio and video creators, both hobbyist and professional. It's supplied with a range of open source software for multimedia creation.

APPENDIX 2
Online resources for help

If you have a problem with Linux or just want to chat about the system with other users, here are the best websites to visit:

http://help.ubuntu.com

The home site for Ubuntu documentation. Here you'll find links to the latest guides for the most recent versions of Ubuntu.

www.ubuntuguide.org

An excellent resource showing you how to perform advanced tasks not covered by the standard documentation. For instance, it shows you how to run virtualisation software such as VirtualBox, add extra graphical effects to your desktop, set up Linux as a thin-client server and much more. Whenever you have a question about doing something specific in Ubuntu, check here first as it will probably be covered.

Desktop Add-ons

There are many add-on icons, themes, wallpapers, 3-D effects, and other customizations available for the GNOME desktop.

Gnome Eye-Candy Resources

- Gnome Look ⚲ has wallpapers, splash screens, icons, and themes for windows managers (including Metacity and Compiz) and other applications.

Metacity

Metacity is the default desktop compositing manager in Gnome. It is lightweight, streamlined and does not have many configurable options, but has multiple themes available at Gnome Look.

Compiz Fusion

Compiz Fusion is available as a separate Windows Manager, to allow advanced desktop effects such as the rotating cube desktop. Many Ubuntu users choose to run Compiz, which is quite fast in Ubuntu. Install:

```
sudo apt-get install compiz compizconfig-settings-manager compiz-fusion-plugins-main compiz-fusion-plugins-extra emerald
```

To change to Compiz as the Window Manager:

- Select Compiz Configuration:
  System -> Preferences -> CompizConfig Settings Manager
  Note: You must logout and log back in for the change to take effect.

Fusion Icon

Fusion Icon is a tray icon that allows you to easily switch between window managers, window decorators, and gives you quick access to the Compiz Settings Manager. This allows quick toggling of 3-D desktop effects (that may not be compatible with some applications).

www.ubuntuguide.org contains a wealth of advanced documentation.

www.ubuntuforums.org

Busy and friendly forums for Ubuntu users, with over 50,000 active members. This site is divided into several sub-forums – installation, hardware support, networking, multimedia and much more. Along with the help forum there are places to discuss development of Ubuntu Linux, the design of the desktop and games. This is by far the best place to get help with Ubuntu; it's totally free to sign up.

www.linuxquestions.org

A broader Linux forum that covers all distributions, and not just Ubuntu. If you need help with a different distro or nobody can help you on the Ubuntu forums, it's well worth posting a message here. You can also ask questions about programming and other variants of Unix.

Forum	Last Post	Threads	Posts
2009 LinuxQuestions.org Members Choice Awards This forum is for the 2009 LinuxQuestions.org Members Choice Awards. You can now vote for your favorite products of 2009. This is your chance to be heard! Voting ends on February 9th.	Browser of the Year by leopard Yesterday 01:49 AM	28	1,499
Linux			
Linux - Newbie This forum is for members that are new to Linux. Just starting out and have a question? If it is not in the man pages or the how-to's this is the place!	sed remove string until final... by nonamenobody Today 06:32 AM	117,693	640,198
Linux - Software This forum is for Software issues. Having a problem installing a new program? Want to know which application is best for the job? Post your question in this forum. Sub-Forums: Linux - Games, Linux - Kernel	Nucleo doesn't compile by MTK358 Today 07:23 AM	136,888	597,935
Linux - Hardware This forum is for Hardware issues. Having trouble installing a piece of hardware? Want to know if that peripheral is compatible with Linux? Sub-Forums: Linux - Embedded	Sound does not work with... by allend Today 07:18 AM	56,772	255,756
Linux - Laptop and Netbook Having a problem installing or configuring Linux on your laptop? Need help running Linux on your netbook? This forum is for you. This forum is for any topics relating to Linux and either traditional laptops or netbooks (such as the Asus EEE PC, Everex CloudBook or MSI Wind).	gateway nv5927u i5 m430... by mrmnemo Yesterday 09:41 PM	13,259	62,187
Linux - Mobile This forum is for the discussion of all topics relating to Mobile Linux. This includes Android, LiMo, Maemo, LiPS, Moblin, Openmoko, Ubuntu Mobile, Open Mobile Alliance and other similar projects and products.	Why did you switch to Linux? by CoderMan Yesterday 06:55 PM	172	756
Linux - Security This forum is for all security related questions. Questions, tips, system compromises, firewalls, etc. are all included here.	How to remove script... by unSpawn Today 05:27 AM	15,011	80,371
Linux - Server This forum is for the discussion of Linux Software used in a server related context.	I want your advice helped me... by okcomputer44 Today 07:09 AM	17,011	73,956

At www.linuxquestions.org you can post questions to thousands of other Linux users and get help very quickly.

⚠ Forum posts

A note on forum posts: it's best to provide as much information as possible in your first post, even if it appears to be overkill. Too many people say things like 'Help! My screen resolution is wrong' and get no response. For other users to help, they need to know the exact version of Linux you're using, what hardware you have, what you've tried to do and any error messages you've seen.

The more specifics you provide, the easier it is for others to help. It can be frustrating if something isn't working properly, but all of the people on these forums are helping in their spare time – nobody is paid – so if you don't get the exact help you need, just try another forum. Good luck!

APPENDIX 3
Essential commands

Here are the most important commands that you can enter at the Linux command line, what they do, and examples of usage:

cat – Concatenate (output) the contents of a file. Example: 'cat file.txt' to view the contents of a text file. You can append one file onto another using the '>>' redirection operator: 'cat file1 >> file2' will append the contents of file1 on to file2.

cd – Change directory. You can switch to a directory inside the current one by providing its name, or switch to a directory anywhere on the filesystem with the full path. Entering 'cd' on its own puts you into your home directory. Example: 'cd /etc/X11'.

cp – Copy a file or several files. Example: 'cp file1 file2' copies file1 to file2. If you specify multiple files, the second parameter has to be a directory: 'cp file1 file2 file3 directory1/'.

df – Shows free disk space. This displays the amount of data occupying drives currently mounted on to the system (eg your hard drive, any connected USB thumb drives etc). Use the '-h' option for human-readable sizes.

dmesg – Prints a list of all system messages since the computer was booted. You will see messages from the kernel along with individual applications. This is worth checking if you suspect something is wrong; if you have a problem and post a message on a website forum, other readers may want to see the last few lines of output from this command.

du – Shows the disk space usage for a particular directory. Entered on its own it shows the usage for the current directory (and its subdirectories). Pass the '-h' option for human-readable sizes. Example: 'du -hc dir1/ dir2/ dir3/' shows the disk space usage for the three specified directories, and '-c' prints a complete total at the end.

exit – Exits the current command line session, or, if called from a script, terminates the script. A handy short cut: when you're using an interactive session at the command line, press Ctrl+D to exit (without having to type the command).

free – Shows free (available) memory. Press the '-m' option to view it in megabytes. Note: Linux caches disk activity in RAM for high performance, so don't worry if the first line indicates that most RAM is used. See the second line, '-/+ buffers/cache' for the true value.

grep – A powerful text searching tool. You can use 'grep' to find words or phrases in text files. Example: 'grep "hamster" *' will search for the word 'hamster' in all files in the current directory. Use '-r' to recurse into multiple directories and '-i' for case-insensitive searches.

halt – Shut down the computer. It needs to be run as the root (administrator) user: 'sudo halt'.

kill – Terminates a process/program. You need to follow this with the number of the process to kill – the process ID (or PID). Use the 'ps' command to find the PID of the process you want to stop. If 'kill' doesn't work on its own (asking the program to stop itself), use the '-9' flag: 'kill -9 23414'. This forces the process to stop without asking it.

less – A text-file viewer. Example: 'less README.TXT' shows the text file; navigate using the cursor keys and press Q to quit. Hit '/' and then type a word to search for it. You can view the output of any command using 'less' with the pipe '|' symbol: 'dmesg | less'.

locate – Find a file on your filesystem. Example: 'locate xorg. conf'. This is very fast but uses a database that's rebuilt every day, so it can get out of date. For slower (but always up-to-date) searches use 'find / -name xorg.conf'.

ls – List directory contents. This shows the files in the current directory, or, if a directory is specified, the files in that directory. Example: 'ls -lah' lists in long (detailed) format all files (including hidden ones) with human-readable file sizes.

man – View the manual page for a particular command. This provides detailed information on the options you can use with a command. Use the cursor keys to scroll through the document and the Q key to quit the manual viewer.

mkdir – Make a new directory. Example: 'mkdir mypics'. If you want to make a series of nested directories, use the '-p' option: 'mkdir -p mypics/photos/yakutsk'.

mv – Moves a file from one place to another. Example: 'mv folder/file1 /usr/bin/file2'. You can use 'mv' to rename a file in the current directory: 'mv oldfilename.txt newfilename.txt'. If you specify multiple files, the second parameter has to be a directory.

nano – Edit a text file. This is useful for editing system configuration files. Use Ctrl+O to save (output) a file and Ctrl+X to exit. More keybindings are listed at the bottom of the screen. For files outside of your home directory, you will have to run the command as the root user: 'sudo nano /etc/hosts'.

ps – Displays a list of the currently running processes. On its own, this command will show the processes that were launched by the current user – ie the programs you're running. 'ps ax' displays a complete list of every process running on the system.

rm – Removes a file or directory. Example: 'rm file1'. If you want to remove a directory, you need to pass the '-r' option to 'rm', to tell it to do a recursive removal, eg 'rm -r photos/'. To remove all files in a directory enter 'rm *'.

sh – Run a script. On its own this will just start a new shell, but with a filename it will run it as a shell script. Example: 'sh do-backup.sh'.

startx – If you find yourself in text mode without a graphical display, this will start the X Window System.

sudo – Run ('do') a command as the 'su'peruser (root, the administrator). Some important operations – such as installing programs – affect files outside of your home directory, and therefore require administrator access. Example: 'sudo apt-get install program'. You will be prompted for your password the first time you run a sudo command (although your password is stored for a while afterwards).

tar – An archiving utility. Use 'tar xfv filename' to extract archives that end in .gz or .bz2. To create an archive from a directory, use 'tar cfvz myfiles.tgz mydir/'.

top – Display the most resource-intensive processes on the system in a table format. You can see the amount of RAM each process is using in the 'RES' (resident memory) column, and the processor occupation under '%CPU'. Press Q to quit.

uname – Print the name of the OS you're using. On its own this will just be 'Linux', but with the '-a' option it tells you the exact kernel version you're running among other information. It's worth including this in any forum posts if you're asking for help.

unzip – Use this to extract .zip files. Example: 'unzip archive.zip'.

w – This single-letter command provides lots of information: it shows you how long the system has been running for, the load average (how much the system's resources are being stressed), and who is logged in.

APPENDIX 4
Glossary of Linux terms

Here are explanations for some of the words and phrases you're likely to come across as you use Linux:

BIOS – The Basic Input/Output System program. Every PC includes a BIOS, which is the first thing loaded when the machine turns on. The BIOS performs some hardware checks and then attempts to load a boot loader from any media it can find (hard drive, CD/DVD drive etc). Once the Linux kernel is loaded the BIOS services are no longer needed so it is ignored.

Boot loader – The program that runs on the bare metal of your PC before anything else is loaded, and then goes on to load the Linux kernel. Ubuntu uses GRUB for this purpose; some other distributions use LILO.

The GRUB bootloader is the default in most distros, and includes graphical and text-based modes.

Codec – A program that deciphers a multimedia file format for viewing or listening. Due to software patents and copyright concerns, some codecs such as DVD playback cannot be freely distributed to everywhere in the world. Ubuntu doesn't include DVD playback software on the CD as a result.

Compiler – The program that turns source code into binary format for the CPU to execute. On Linux, the C and C++ compiler is GCC from the GNU project.

Dependency – A library or other piece of software that a program requires. For instance, the GTK toolkit library is a dependency of the Gnome desktop.

Desktop environment – The software that provides the panels, titlebars, widgets and utilities in your Linux installation. In Ubuntu this is Gnome, but other desktops such as KDE and Xfce are available too. Contrast with window managers.

Xfce is a lightweight alternative to the Gnome and KDE desktop environments.

Directory – The technical term for what is represented on the desktop as a folder. In Linux, directories are separated by slashes – eg /usr/bin/. Directories can be written as 'dir' or 'dir/' but the trailing slash is best used for clarity (to distinguish it from a file).

Distribution – aka 'distro'. This is a bootable and (usually) installable compilation of the Linux kernel and applications. Anyone can make a distribution: Ubuntu is the most popular and included with this book.

Filesystem – A chunk of storage space on a device. In a typical Linux installation, your hard drive contains a partition in ext3 format (the way files are laid out on the partition), and the filesystem with all operating system files and your personal files are stored inside that.

glibc – The GNU C library. This is the critical collection of code that all programs written in C use (see 'library'definition).

GNU – GNU'S Not Unix, the project started in the mid-1980s by Richard Stallman. Its goal was to create a complete Unix system with totally open, free and modifiable source code, to provide a more community-spirited alternative to the closed, commercial flavours of Unix that were available at the time. The GNU team didn't do much work on a kernel for the operating system, though, so when the Linux kernel arrived (written by Linus Torvalds) it turned out to be an ideal fit. The system we use today could technically be called GNU/Linux for this reason.

Grok – A term widely used among Linux users and (especially) developers. This comes from a book by sci-fi author Robert A. Heinlein, *Stranger in a Strange Land*, and describes the process of becoming knowledgeable about a subject and finding it inspiring and entertaining at the same time. For instance: 'I really grok Python programming' – I really enjoy learning and exploring Python.

Home directory – The directory (folder) where your personal files are stored. This is /home/username/, eg /home/fred/. Whenever you create new user accounts, their home directories will be created in /home/.

Your home folder is accessible in Ubuntu via the Places menu at the top.

Kernel – The core component of Linux. The kernel is loaded by the boot loader, and talks to your hardware, manages memory and switches between running programs for multitasking. In Ubuntu the kernel file is /boot/vmlinuz- followed by the version number.

Library – A collection of code that other programs can use. To save space and minimise duplication, Linux programs try to share as many libraries as possible. For instance, there is an XML parsing library (libxml2) that all programs which handle XML can use – they don't need their own versions.

Link – A file that points to another file. There are 'symbolic links' (aka 'symlinks') and 'hard links', and these are much like short cuts in Windows. Links allow multiple filenames to point to the same file.

Log file – A text file containing status messages from a program. In Linux the most important one is /var/log/syslog, which can be useful for diagnostics if something appears to be malfunctioning.

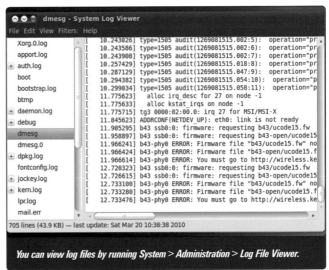

You can view log files by running System > Administration > Log File Viewer.

Module – Many features of the Linux kernel are implemented as modular, standalone pieces of code that the kernel can load when it needs them. Most hardware drivers are implemented as modules. Some programs such as VirtualBox load modules into the kernel to get low-level access to hardware.

Mount – The process of attaching a drive to the Linux filesystem is called mounting. For instance, when you plug in a USB key, the kernel looks for a recognisable filesystem on it, and then presents that as accessible (mounts it) in /media/(device name). You also get an icon on the desktop.

OSS – Open Source Software. Sometimes written FLOSS (Free, Libre Open Source Software. The Libre is there to show that it's free as in freedom, and not just as in price).

Package – A file containing a piece of Linux software. Packages contain the executable binary program code along with documentation, images, scripts etc. On Ubuntu and other Debian-based distros package filenames end in .deb. Some other distros use .rpm packages, an alternative format.

Partition – A portion of your hard drive. On a typical new Windows PC you usually have one large partition filling the entire drive in Windows NTFS format. When you install Linux, you can resize the Windows partition down to make room for the Linux partition(s).

With System > Administration > Disk Utility you can view and edit the partitions on your drive(s).

Process – A piece of code being executed on your system. In most cases each running program will be a single process, but some programs create multiple processes. Use the 'ps ax' command to list them.

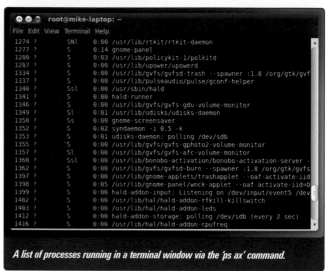

A list of processes running in a terminal window via the 'ps ax' command.

Patch – A text file that contains a list of updates between one version and another of a program. A patch only contains the differences between two files (or a collection of files), which is why it is sometimes also known as a 'diff'. This also means that the patch file is relatively small compared to the original, full compilation of files – for instance, the Linux kernel source code is over 60MB, but when new versions are released the patch files tend to only be a few megabytes.

Ping – This term originates from the 'ping' command line utility, which checks to see whether or not a machine is accessible on the network: eg 'ping google.com'. Ping sends data packets to the machine and tells you whether or not the remote machine has responded. If it doesn't respond, the machine may have crashed or lost power. Recently ping has become a general verb in the Linux world meaning to find out if someone is available/active, eg: 'Have you heard from Dave recently?' – 'No, I'll ping him and see if he has the files ready.'

Port – This has two meanings. A 'port of Linux' is a version of Linux designed to run on a different type of machine – eg a video game console. In networking, a port is a numbered 'hole' for communication to and from the outside world: eg if you run a web server, other machines will connect to yours via port 80.

Release – A version of a Linux distribution. If someone says that they are using the latest release of Ubuntu, for instance, it means that they are running the most recent version that was made available on the Internet. Linux distribution releases tend to arrive much more quickly than with Windows or Mac OS X – in the case of Ubuntu there's a new release every six months. You can upgrade to a new release over the Internet using the Upgrade Manager or by getting hold of a new Ubuntu CD, booting it and installing it from scratch.

Repository – A collection of packages, usually on the Internet, which include the dependencies required to run them. You can add repositories to your Ubuntu installation to get new software as it's released.

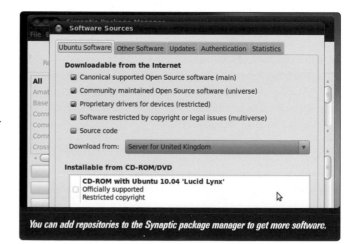

You can add repositories to the Synaptic package manager to get more software.

Root – The administrator or 'superuser'. You can run commands as the root user by entering 'sudo' followed by the command, or launch a full root session with 'sudo bash'. Root's personal files are stored in /root/.

Root directory – This is the top-level directory in Linux, from which all other directories start, somewhat like the C: drive on a single-partition Windows machine. The root directory is just a slash ('/') and other directories inside it are noted as /bin/, /var/ and so forth.

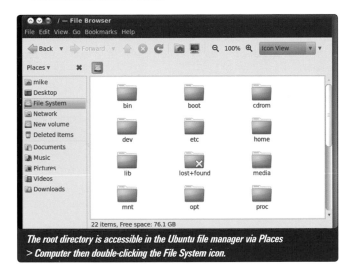

The root directory is accessible in the Ubuntu file manager via Places > Computer then double-clicking the File System icon.

Shell – Another name for the command prompt. In Ubuntu and most Linux distributions, the default shell program is called Bash, but others such as KSH and ZSH are available. Bash lets you enter commands and it can also run scripts.

Source code – The original, human-readable recipe for a program. Programs written in C and C++ source code, such as the Linux kernel, X Window System, glibc and Gnome desktop environment, are compiled into a non-human-readable binary format that the CPU understands.

```
/*
 * Return the offset into page `page_nr' of the last valid
 * byte in that page, plus one.
 */
static unsigned
ext2_last_byte(struct inode *inode, unsigned long page_nr)
{
        unsigned last_byte = inode->i_size;

        last_byte -= page_nr << PAGE_CACHE_SHIFT;
        if (last_byte > PAGE_CACHE_SIZE)
                last_byte = PAGE_CACHE_SIZE;
        return last_byte;
}

static int ext2_commit_chunk(struct page *page, loff_t pos, unsigned len)
{
        struct address_space *mapping = page->mapping;
        struct inode *dir = mapping->host;
        int err = 0;

        dir->i_version++;
        block_write_end(NULL, mapping, pos, len, len, page, NULL);
```

Source code is often in plain text format and can be modified in any editor.

TCP/IP – The Transmission Control Protocol/Internet Protocol. This controls the way computers communicate with one another across the Internet.

Terminal – A command line window. In Ubuntu this is in Applications > Accessories > Terminal.

Unix – A hugely powerful, multi-user, industrial-strength operating system that started life in the 1970s. Unix was forked (split off) by various companies and used on high-end servers. Linux is heavily based on the design of Unix, although it doesn't use Unix code. Examples of commercial Unix still in use today include Sun/Oracle's Solaris and IBM's AIX.

Vi – An extremely terse, difficult to grasp text editor that is often mentioned in Linux and Unix documentation because it's included with every distro. Vim, an enhanced version of Vi, is hugely powerful but we recommend that most users get started with the much simpler Nano (see the command appendix).

Window manager – A small piece of software that communicates with the X Window System and provides the surroundings for programs. Desktop environments include their own window managers, but you will find smaller, standalone ones too, such as IceWM and Fluxbox. See www.xwinman.org for a list.

Fluxbox is a minimalist window manager favoured by many Linux power-users.

X Window System – Also known as X and X11. This is the base graphical layer of Linux, which communicates with the kernel and your graphics card to give you a bitmapped display. Desktop environments (eg Gnome) and applications then talk to the 'X server' to display their output on the screen.

LINUX MANUAL
Index

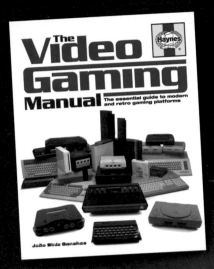

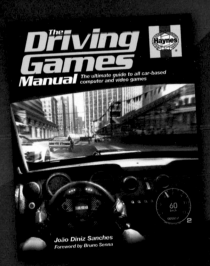

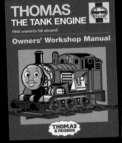

MAR 2012